# LOST RAIL
# OF
# MIDDLESEX

Mike Hall

COUNTRYSIDE BOOKS
NEWBURY, BERKSHIRE

First Published 2003
© Mike Hall 2003

COUNTRYSIDE BOOKS
3 Catherine Road
Newbury, Berkshire

To view our complete range of books,
please visit us at
www.countrysidebooks.co.uk

ISBN 1 85306 802 0

The cover picture shows the improved Director class loco. They were
blessed with impressive names such as Ypres, Somme and Jutland.
Eleven were built in 1919 including nos 501-511.
(From an original painting by Colin Doggett)

Produced through MRM Associates Ltd., Reading
Typeset by Techniset Typesetters, Newton-le-Willows
Printed by Woolnough Bookbinding Ltd., Irthlingborough

# CONTENTS

# ACKNOWLEDGEMENTS

I would like to thank the staff of the various local reference
libraries and custodians of local history collections who patiently
and efficiently dealt with my many requests for archive photos
and documents, also to those kind folk who responded to my
requests for information in local newspapers and also the
copyright owners of photographs. I would particularly like to
thank Mike Stanbury of the East Anglian Railway Society and
Leslie Oppitz for help in tracking down some of the photographs. I owe a special debt to my wife, Linda, who drew the
maps. Any errors are mine, not hers.

# ABBREVIATIONS

The following abbreviations are used in this book:

| | |
|---|---|
| CLR | Central London Railway |
| ECR | Eastern Counties Railway |
| ELR | East London Railway |
| GCR | Great Central Railway |
| GER | Great Eastern Railway |
| GNR | Great Northern Railway |
| GWR | Great Western Railway |
| LMS | London, Midland and Scottish Railway |
| LNER | London & North Eastern Railway |
| LNWR | London & North Western Railway |
| LR&A | Latimer Road & Acton Railway |
| LSWR | London & South Western Railway |
| LT | London Transport |
| MDR | Metropolitan District Railway |
| MWB | Metropolitan Water Board |
| NLR | North London Railway |
| N&SWJR | North & South West Junction Railway |
| WLE | West London Extension |

*This book is dedicated
to the memory of my father who loved railways.*

The expeditions by North London trains
To dim forgotten stations, wooden shacks
On oil-lit flimsy platforms among fields
As yet unbuilt on, deep in Middlesex ...

There was no station, north to Finsbury Park,
To Barking eastwards, Clapham Common south,
No temporary platform in the west
Among the Actons and the Ealings, where
We had not once alighted ...

From *Summoned By Bells* by Sir John Betjeman

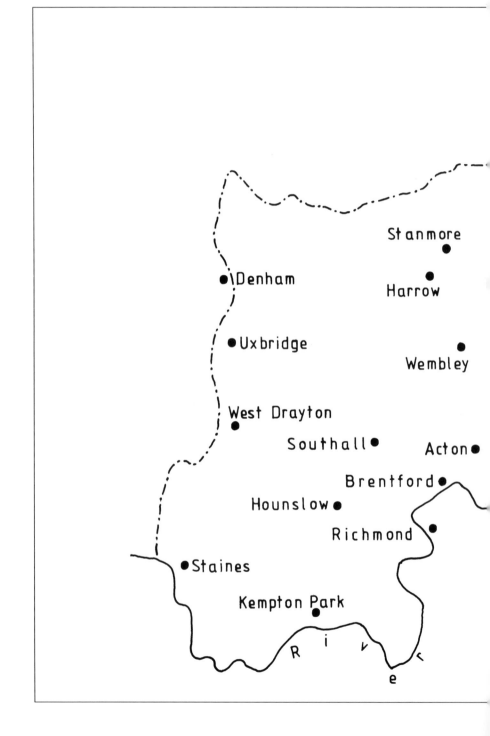

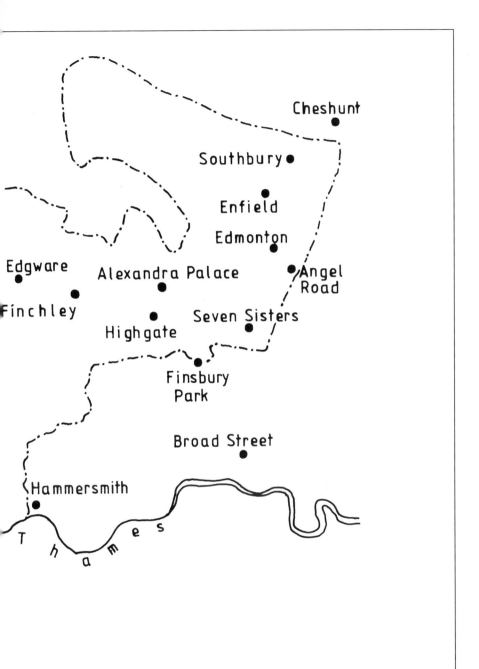

# Introduction

A rather unpromising footpath leads from the Piccadilly Line bridge over Spring Grove, Hounslow, in the general direction of Hounslow bus garage. No-one much uses it as it squeezes uncomfortably behind the back garden fences of North Drive. To the right an overgrown embankment marks the course of the former Metropolitan District Railway's line to its long-dismantled Hounslow Town terminus. At the bus station a metal plaque put up by the local historical society informs those waiting passengers who might be interested (and the majority are probably not) that they are queuing on the site of the old station. A quarter of a mile to the north a sleek electric train bound for Heathrow Central glides away from the platform at Hounslow East.

The former county of Middlesex, with its complex network of main line, suburban and London Underground railways snaking out of the capital, might seem unlikely territory for the seeker of lost railways yet there are a surprising number to be found, even in the most densely built-up districts. Some, like the little loop that took excited punters to the futuristic delights of the Empire Exhibition at Wembley in the 1920s, have left little trace. The course of others, like the railway to Uxbridge (Vine Street) which lasted into the late 1960s, can be identified by the tell-tale linear developments of modern houses or the occasional bridge parapet or overgrown footpath. A few, like the one from Finsbury Park to Highgate, have become attractive footpaths. Out in the semi-rural fringes on the borders of Buckinghamshire were single-track branches to Staines (West) and Uxbridge (High Street) that seemed to have remained backwaters for all their uneventful years. Yet others, such as the line that snaked its way down from Palace Gates and Wood Green to Seven Sisters and on to North Woolwich, were vital transport routes to their working-class passengers for generations until closure.

On lines that are still open a fragment of platform or a blocked-up street entrance may be all that remains of ghost stations such as St Ann's Road or Junction Road (both on the Gospel Oak to

*Uxbridge (Vine Street) c1930. (Stations UK)*

Barking line), or Staines High Street on the Windsor branch.

There is still a lot to be seen if you know where to look. Out-of-date Ordnance Survey maps and A to Z street atlases show you where to go and even on the most modern maps the route of a long-defunct railway can often be traced in the suburban road pattern. I spent a fascinating year tramping obscure suburban streets, crashing through the undergrowth of the rural fringes where Middlesex meets Buckinghamshire and looking for those tell-tale signs: a bridge parapet, a length of railway fencing, a parade of shops next to what was once a busy station. I hope I have not missed much, although I am aware of a few gaps – I have not attempted to sort out the maze of lines linking the City and the Docks between Broad Street and the River Lea, for example; these need a book to themselves.

Mike Hall

# 1
# The Slow Way To Staines

*The Staines & West Drayton Railway*

*Push-pull steam train in Staines West station in the 1950s.*
*(Spelthorne Museum)*

Staines might seem to many the ultimate Southern Electric destination, served by a reliable and frequent suburban service from Waterloo, westbound trains then fanning out from Staines Central station to a variety of destinations including Guildford, Reading, Windsor and Weybridge.

But there used to be another way of getting there by rail, a single-track line traversing moor and meadow, a rural Great Western branch that slipped almost apologetically into the back of town, a district that even now seems curiously remote from suburbia.

The London & South Western Railway had reached Staines from Waterloo in 1848, reviving a market town that had been in eclipse since the old coaching days, but the businessmen of Staines wanted a rail link to the main line from Paddington which passed by just six miles to the north. After various schemes that came to nothing, the Staines & West Drayton Railway Company was set up and work was commenced on a single track leading south from a junction with the GWR at West Drayton, passing close to the old town of Colnbrook, famous for its coaching inns, on the Bath Road.

Money was tight and this gave rise to one of the unique curiosities of the GWR Staines branch, what can only be described as a second-hand station! The terminus was to be in Moor Lane on the northern edge of the town close to a well-known industrial establishment, the Mustard Mill. The mill's owner was one John Finch Esq and his house, called Moor House but also known locally as the Mill House, had been built in 1820. Someone had the bright idea of buying this property and converting it into the terminus station for the branch. Mr Finch was persuaded to sell and the platforms, canopies, tracks and buffers duly appeared in the front garden of Moor House which, little altered externally, became Staines station (the suffix 'West' was not added until 1949, after Nationalisation). The mill itself was demolished to make way for the goods yard.

The Staines & West Drayton Railway opened in 1884/5. The proposals for the line had included a link passing below the GWR main line at West Drayton, allowing trains from Staines to run through onto the Uxbridge branch, but this was never proceeded with. Opposition from the LSWR scuppered plans to run into the larger company's station at Staines, hence the decision to terminate the branch in Moor Lane, short of the town centre. At first Colnbrook was the only intermediate station, built north of the Bath Road (which was crossed on the level) and east of the village. There was a signal box and a goods yard as well as a passing loop. In 1895, however, a station was opened on Staines Moor for the use of soldiers travelling to the Metropolitan Rifle Ranges just three minutes' brisk march down the lane. The

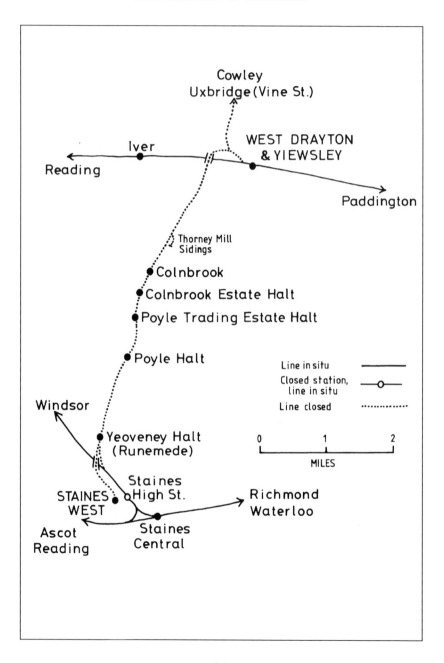

*The wilds of Staines Moor, Yeoveney Halt. The M25 now runs across the fields to the left of the line). (Spelthorne Museum)*

new station bore the unlikely name of Runemede Range because the Metropolitan Rifle Range Company Limited had previously had its butts at Coopers Hill, Runnymede near Egham, from where they had been relocated in 1891.

Staines Moor was obviously the place for target practice in Victorian times because the impressively-named 44th Middlesex Rifle Volunteer Corps had had their range nearby from 1862 to 1892 when it was closed following a petition to the War Office from none other than the Staines & West Drayton Railway Company, who were, it seems, concerned for the safety of their passengers. Presumably the Runemede ranges were considered to be at a safe distance!

They continued in operation until the early 1930s, possibly providing some income for the Great Western Railway which had absorbed the Staines & West Drayton in 1900. Even after this date the little platform, renamed Yeoveney Halt in November 1935 (after being known for the previous year as the plain but

15

geographically hopelessly inaccurate Runemede), remained open almost until the line closed in 1965.

It was never an impressive structure. There was simply a 20ft long wooden platform with no shelter, just a seat and a lamp-post and back fence. The only access was by the field path from the range pavilion in Moor Lane. Trains stopped by request, but once it got dark intending passengers had to raise the lamp up on the post provided. This was the signal to the driver to stop. Occasionally you nearly weren't noticed and the driver had to stop the train and reverse back into the gloom. This anachronism could not last and Yeoveney Halt was closed 'due to the cost of repair' on 13th May 1962.

For most of its life the Great Western's Staines line was little more than a fairly insignificant branch served by a single engine and carriage push-pull train. It was always worked with the engine at the Staines end, pushing the carriage towards West Drayton and pulling it back to Staines. It must have been a tranquil journey in those days, before the area was blasted by the sounds of jets coming in to land at Heathrow, gravel

*Horse power – shunting in the Staines lino works. (Spelthorne Museum)*

pits encroached and the meadows were ploughed up to build the M25.

There was always significant freight traffic on the branch though. The linoleum factory at Staines was a particular source of revenue. Linoleum, from the Latin *linum* (linen), *oleum* (oil) but usually shortened to just lino, was a very popular and hard-wearing floor covering right up to the 1960s. It was invented by Frederick Walton in 1860 and he established his works (the world's first) in a former calico-printing works alongside the River Colne at Staines. Its connection to the GWR line in 1887 involved the construction of a bridge across the river and a complicated network of internal interconnecting lines. Raw materials brought in by rail included linseed oil, resins, cork and pigments. These were mixed and pressed into the oxidised oil on coarse canvas between steam-heated rollers. The process also needed large quantities of coal so the railway was kept busy.

At times of national emergency the little branch assumed somewhat greater importance. The Staines Linoleum factory's use for military purposes during the First World War and the opening of various camps around Staines at that time produced extra traffic and revenue. On 11th July 1927 Stanwell Moor & Poyle Halt was opened a short distance south of Colnbrook, partly to serve the Poyle Explosive Works. One wonders about the wisdom of steam engines chuffing past this potentially lethal establishment, but no-one seems to have been concerned at the time. In 1939 a connecting line to the Southern Railway route was constructed across Staines Moor. This was part of a scheme to provide an alternative safer route by which freight trains might avoid London in the event of heavy bombing of the capital. The idea was to bring traffic from the North and Midlands round into the marshalling yards at Feltham or towards the South East should the railway bridges in the London area be blocked or destroyed.

The diversionary track proved its worth from September 1940 but was disused after the war. In 1960 there was a scheme to reopen it and divert the branch trains into Staines Central, the former LSWR station. This would have eliminated the need to build a bridge to carry the new Staines bypass (the A30) across the branch track. It would also have resulted in easier

17

*Staines West station. A few years before closure, a diesel railcar arrives from West Drayton. (Spelthorne Museum)*

interchange for passengers who would no longer have to cross the town centre on foot from West to Central or vice versa. Perhaps surprisingly, there was local opposition to the plan and it was abandoned – a foretaste of the opposition mounted at the start of the 21st century when the privately-financed Central Railways Company proposed a new freight line linking the Midlands to the Channel Tunnel, which would have crossed part of Staines Moor.

Perhaps the opponents in 1960 would have better used their energies in supporting anything that might have made the Staines West branch more convenient and economically viable because the infamous Beeching Plan listed the passenger service for closure. This was despite some recent attempts to raise revenue from workers in the factory estates that had mush-roomed in the flat fields around Colnbrook after the establish-ment of London Airport from 1946. In January 1954 Poyle Trading Estate Halt, an unglamorous utilitarian concrete structure, was opened. Trains stopped there at rush hours, but

18

at other times by request only. Yet another halt was opened on 1st May 1961. Colnbrook Estate Halt, another bleak, bare platform, making a total of four station stops in less than two miles, must have been one of the shortest-lived railway stations in the country!

The end came on 27th March 1965 when the platform at Staines West was unprecedentedly crowded with those witnessing the final departure for West Drayton. To the traditional accompaniment of exploding detonators the diesel multiple unit departed bearing a home-made placard reading: 'The end is nigh, prepare to meet thy bus. Born 1885, died 1965, it's over, The End.'

It was not quite the end. Although the link to the lino works had been taken up in 1957 there was still substantial goods traffic. An oil storage depot had been constructed in 1964 on the site of the former goods yard at Staines West. Freight trains from Purfleet traversed the branch and there were also oil trains to depots at Colnbrook and Thorney Mills, south of West Drayton. The left hand did not seem to know what the right hand was doing. Even as the closure of the passenger service was being announced locally, the derelict goods yard was redeveloped for this terminal. The track south of Colnbrook therefore had to be retained for a freight service that ran about once a week in the winter and barely once a month in summer.

But the line was not to survive intact through to its centenary in 1985. The trackbed between Colnbrook and Staines lay in the path of the projected London Orbital Motorway, the M25. In 1980 a new link was constructed, connecting the oil storage terminals with the Southern Region's Staines to Windsor line so that it could continue to be accessed by rail.

On 24th January 1981 the last train ran to Staines West along the branch from West Drayton. It was a special excursion from Paddington, operated by a diesel multiple unit and bearing the same placard that had graced the final regular passenger train in 1965. Within days the line across Staines Moor was dismantled and the railway bridges opposite the Swan public house in Moor Lane were demolished.

Staines West, that curious second-hand station, survives though. It had been registered as a Listed Building in 1977 and

*Staines West station house has had an eventful history and remains in use as offices. (Author)*

*Rear view of Staines West station. (Author)*

*Some track remains in place at Staines West. This view is looking southwards from the bridge carrying the footpath from Moor Lane towards Poyle. (Author)*

21

this should have given it statutory protection but it had already become derelict. It was sold by British Rail to Spelthorne Borough Council for £1 and in about nine months, from July 1981 to April 1982, converted into prestigious offices.

The 'off-the-peg' station house is still recognisable but of the platforms and sidings there is now no sign, an up-market housing development having been built on the site. However, the observant explorer heading north from the station along Moor Lane will see numbers 1, 2 and 3 Great Western Cottages on the right beyond the Jewson builders' yard. It is said that one of the regular locomotive crew lived here and used to climb over the fence at the end of his garden to go and light up the engine! A little further on, before Moor Lane is crossed by the Staines bypass, a footpath signposted 'Stanwell Moor' leads off to the right. This rises to cross the trackbed of the branch as well as the Wraysbury River and the Windsor line. A short length of track and a set of points remain in place, visible from the south side of the bridge, looking back towards the terminus. From the north side the more modern bridge carrying the bypass blocks the view but the separate arch for the branch track – the one that would not have been needed if the 1960 scheme had been proceeded with – is clearly visible.

Further along Moor Lane, nearly opposite the Swan pub, in an area of the town that seems quite rural, the branch's embankment is clearly visible to the right. The motorway has truncated Moor Lane just beyond its bridge over the Windsor line but a wide surfaced footpath leads across Staines Moor towards Poyle. If the incessant roar from the M25 on the left could be ignored, the eerie mystery of these damp meadows would still be felt on a winter's evening. A line of trees and the tell-tale double row of railway fence-posts reveal the route of the old railway. The more intrepid can take a muddy footpath to the right and find the site of Yeoveney Halt, marked by a row of concrete posts, nearly forty years after the last passenger raised the lamp at dusk to bring the branch train to a stop, seemingly miles from the nearest habitation.

The tarmac path leads on towards Poyle. The track of the old railway comes in from the right at an angle, its route blocked by a gate. From here to Poyle it is totally obliterated by the

*Old station house and level crossing, Colnbrook. (Author)*

motorway. The keen explorer is welcome to follow the path to Poyle but it has little to recommend it. Horton Lane, which leads into Stanwell Moor, has to be crossed with care on a blind bend and then there are subways under the slip roads and a footbridge over the motorway at junction 14. The Poyle trading estate which then has to be passed through is a litter-strewn area, of interest only to devotees of late 20th century light industry and low-flying aircraft. The only older buildings, the attractive Golden Cross pub and two farms on Poyle Road, seem somewhat incongruous. The railway, with its numerous short-lived halts, ran down the eastern boundary of the industrial estate but is largely inaccessible and untraceable.

Colnbrook, with its attractive old coaching inns on the Bath Road, comes as something of a relief but Colnbrook station lay a mile to the east back in Poyle. The old station house is still to be seen by the level crossing and the rails remain in place northwards from here to the main line. A single track crosses

*The track of the GWR Staines West branch still survives (just) as far south as the former Colnbrook station. View looking north from the level crossing with station house on the left. (Author)*

the road at a level crossing over the Bath Road south of the station. There are warning signs and lights that presumably could still operate but there are fairly permanent-looking fences across the railway on both sides of the road and vehicles parked on the line on the south side where a car dealer's premises now exist.

Curiously a prominent sign by this sad stub end of track at Colnbrook station announces that the line is part of the grandiosely-titled 'English Welsh & Scottish Railway', one of the more improbable outcomes of rail privatisation. At least there is evidence here of some freight traffic being kept off the congested road network.

The surviving single line can be seen from the A4 Colnbrook bypass, from the M4/M25 interchange (if you know where to look and are not driving!) and also from Thorney Mill Road between West Drayton and Langley, although the blighted ravaged scenery in this area may limit such an excursion to the really dedicated branch-line enthusiast. The junction at West Drayton can be seen in greater comfort from passing trains.

# 2
# Unfinished At Uxbridge

*West Drayton to Vine Street and northwards from Uxbridge High Street*

*Uxbridge (Vine Street) Station. The destination board propped up in the foreground reads 'PADDINGTON'. Through services to London were a feature of this branch. (Hillingdon Library Services)*

## Uxbridge misses out

Somehow Uxbridge had missed out in the Great Railway Game. An important town in coaching days, 'full of inns' according to one 17th century traveller, well-connected to the national canal network and an industrial town of some significance, it had

26

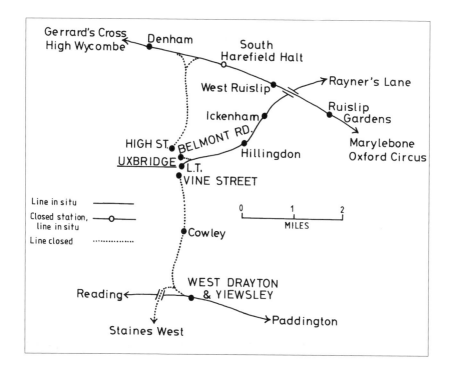

nevertheless been by-passed by the railways. The Great Western main line passed two miles to the south, through West Drayton, in 1848 and much later, in 1897, the joint GWR and Great Central High Wycombe line was to be constructed a similar distance to the north, through Denham.

Uxbridge, on the direct Oxford road, had been too close to London perhaps to have had much of a role as an overnight stopping place for travellers but the traders and innkeepers had nevertheless done well in coaching days. The opening of the GWR line was catastrophic for the town, which faced becoming merely a rural backwater. The only answer was – a Railway for Uxbridge!

Various ambitious schemes were promoted by local interests. The 1845 prospectus of the imposingly-titled Middlesex & Surrey Junction Railway is typical in its florid writing and unfulfilled promises:

'This railway is proposed to commence at Uxbridge, proceed

27

thence to Southall station on the Great Western Railway and thence through Heston to Hounslow. The line proceeds through Whitton, Twickenham, Teddington and Hampton to Kingston and, crossing the Thames, to Kingston station on the South Western Railway, whence it will proceed to and terminate at Epsom.

'The line proposed is perfectly free from engineering difficulties and the towns and places through which it passes or most immediately affects, contain an aggregate population of about 200,000 persons.

'The ordinary traffic between the places proposed to be connected to the line is already sufficiently great to justify the formation of the railway, without reference to the additional traffic inevitably consequent on the facilities afforded by railway communication, almost beyond calculation in so populous a locality, and so near to the Metropolis as this.

'To the inhabitants of Uxbridge this line presents the most direct communication with the Metropolis, adopting the old courses taken by the coaches, viz. through Hillingdon, Hayes, Southall &c., contrasting favourably with the present circuitous route to London by coach or omnibus to West Drayton and thence by the Great Western Railway.

'By means of this line, and of the proposed line from London to Hounslow which this will intersect, Brentford, the county town of Middlesex, and the Thames, will be brought into immediate connection with Uxbridge, the traffic between the last-named towns has hitherto materially helped to produce the large dividends of the Grand Junction Canal.'

Despite all these inducements to potential shareholders, and despite the promoters including local worthies such as 'Henry Pownall Esq. of Spring Grove, Hounslow, Magistrate for Middlesex and Director of the Great Western, Brentford & Central Terminus Junction Railway', this grandiose scheme was just one of the ventures which sank without trace in the years of the so-called 'Railway Mania'.

Yet by the first half of the 20th century Uxbridge would remarkably have three terminus stations, totally disconnected from each other, with a fourth – already closed to railway traffic – thrown in for good measure!

28

# Trains to Vine Street

There were various schemes for lines passing to the north of Uxbridge but the town worthies were not satisfied. They wanted a station in Uxbridge itself and in 1856 a broad gauge branch was opened from West Drayton to a terminus at Vine Street on the southern edge of the town. It was graced with an all-over timber and glass roof, typical of the more important Great Western stations at the time, a feature it was to retain until the 1930s.

The year after the line opened a Mr W.H. Kitchen wrote to the directors of the GWR on behalf of the inhabitants of Cowley, then an isolated village between Uxbridge and West Drayton, to request that a station be provided there. At first they seemed amenable and Mr Kitchen was told as much. But then the Great Man himself spoke; no less a personage than Isambard Kingdom Brunel delivered his opinion that there would be insufficient traffic to justify this. The proposal for a station at Cowley was rejected and the villagers had to wait until 1904 before they were deemed worthy of one. Even so, a county guidebook published in 1906 was still able to describe Cowley as 'a pretty village with

*Cowley station soon after its opening (Hillingdon Library Services)*

several old brick houses screened from the road by walls and ancient trees.' It sounds idyllic.

In 1871 the line was converted to standard gauge and in 1880 the single line was doubled. There seems to have been something of a lack of maintenance at the time because in his official report the Board of Trade inspector, Colonel Yolland, wrote 'I must not omit to call attention to the fact that I noticed several gates at occupation crossings were not closed and in no case did I observe locks on any of the gates. The fencing is very old and requires to be carefully overhauled.'

In 1894 the hours being worked by staff at Vine Street station were described as 'excessive' in the General Manager's report. An average of fourteen hours a day was not untypical. Another junior clerk and an adult porter were added to the station's complement of staff.

The number of people working at places such as Vine Street in the heyday of Britain's railways seems astonishing to a generation brought up in the modern era of bleak utilitarian unmanned stations. An article in the Great Western Railway Journal dated Winter 1995 lists over twenty full-time staff employed there in 1925. Apart from the station master there were two booking clerks, three goods clerks, two ticket collectors, one parcels porter, one porter/signalman, one porter, one horse parcel van man, one waiting room attendant, two goods carters, one leading carter, one motor driver, two goods checkers, two goods porters, two goods shunters, two signalmen and two passenger guards. There were also a number of casual staff. Of course, they would not all have been on duty at once but even so the place must have been swarming!

At Cowley station in the 1930s there was a small kiosk near the entrance run by a Mr & Mrs Newbury. In slack times when there were few customers for refreshments Mr Newbury carried on his other trade, repairing watches – an unusual business to take place on railway property. At Vine Street at about the same time there was a ladies' hairdressers in the station building. This had been set up by two friends called Lucy and Ena and traded as 'Maison Lucena'. The business was later taken over by the wife of the local fishmonger. For the sake of her customers one hopes she did not come to work straight from the fish shop!

A feature of the Vine Street branch until 1939 was the provision of a number of through trains via Paddington and the Metropolitan Railway to the City. The fastest journey time to Paddington was 20 minutes. For a few years at the end of the 19th century there were also through trains between Vine Street and Victoria via Latchmere Junction at Battersea.

Goods traffic was also brisk. One of the best customers in the 1930s was Alfred Buttons, a local wholesaler, whose premises were actually on the site of the first Metropolitan Railway terminus in Belmont Road (of which more later). Among many other items, he shifted substantial quantities of Kellogg's cereals. Such was the volume of his trade that, when the Kellogg's factory was about to close for its annual three weeks summer break, the extra supplies he received to tide him over took the army of goods-handling staff at Vine Street about a week to clear, with their GWR delivery vans working to capacity.

Other local businesses that used the railway were Sandersons, the Bell Punch Company and Harris's, famed for their pies and sausages. An unusual traffic was made up of the barrels of Lamberts caramel, made at their factory in Oxford Road and transferred by rail to Burton on Trent where it was used to colour beer. I wonder if the hardened drinkers of the Midlands realised they were consuming sweetmeats from Middlesex!

# Rails beside the river

When, in 1897, the High Wycombe line was the second major route to bypass Uxbridge there was much local protest. It was recognised by many that the new route was a classic 'spoiling' operation to block a similar scheme by the District Railway. However, to keep the Uxbridge faction sweet, the GWR did agree to build another line into Uxbridge, this time from the north, opened in 1907. The double-track line was served by steam railmotor trains which operated from Ealing and Greenford to Denham where they reversed to trundle down to Uxbridge. Later in the line's history services operated from Gerrard's Cross.

31

There were hopes that this route down the Colne Valley could be linked up with the Vine Street line to make a useful circular route but the prudent Great Western board decided it would be cheaper to stop short at a new and rather basic station in the High Street. If this link had been completed the older Vine Street station would have been left stranded at the end of a short siding and would either have been closed or used as a goods depot.

Some construction work on the proposed link was started – a cutting, an embankment, a 1,275 yard brick viaduct and an iron girder bridge over the High Street were left unfinished. Since the joint District and Metropolitan Railway service on their direct route into the town via Rayner's Lane had begun in 1904 the extra expenditure necessary to complete the Uxbridge circle would have produced little return on the investment.

The junction with the High Wycombe line had curves linking west to Denham and east towards South Harefield but the latter was never used for regular passenger services and the track was lifted as a wartime economy in about 1916. In 1942 part of this link to the main line was restored to serve an oil depot.

*Uxbridge (High Street) station. The dead-end viaduct of the planned extension. Luckily no train ever over-ran the buffer stops at the end of the line! (Hillingdon Library Service)*

32

Construction of the line from Denham was not difficult. The valley of the River Colne provided a very level route. The only problem was the large number of streams that had to be crossed or diverted. At Denham an area of land had to be drained before the embankments could be built. There had been fears in Uxbridge that some well-loved local landmarks would have to be demolished, notably the old Treaty House, built around 1570, but no major demolitions were needed.

An unusual feature of Denham station on the main line was that it had a subway that was above ground level. The reason for this apparent anomaly is the fact that the station was built on a 25-foot-high embankment. The pedestrian subway linking the two platforms tunnelled through this embankment about half-way up. It must have disconcerted unwary passengers who, after descending the steps from the platforms, found themselves still high above the ground in the arch of a bridge under the tracks.

From the junction at Denham, the line ran southwards on an embankment and crossed Fray's River near Denham Lock. Rounding the curve from the main line, engines passed a typical mushroom-shaped GWR water tower, incongruously placed on its own among the watermeadows. Nearby a two-boiler steam pumping station supplied water to the water troughs on the main line at Ruislip. The railway followed the west bank of the river to Uxbridge (High Street) station. It was an abrupt end, the tracks leading through the station onto the truncated bridge of the unbuilt extension. It looked as if the station was waiting to cater for the through traffic which never came.

The girder bridge over the road itself was removed in 1922 but the approach span and the last arches leading to it survived until 1981. There was a rather flimsy-looking wooden station building beside the track; a tea room and other facilities were built at ground level.

# High Street memories

An unusual event held at this quiet terminus on 2nd April 1926 was, according to a report in the *Railway Gazette*, a demonstration of 'A Quicker Method of Unloading Roadstone from Railway Wagons by the use of Smith's Patent Hoppers'.

This was what nowadays would be called a commercial presentation put on by the manufacturers and attended by representatives of the GWR, LMS, LNER and Southern Railway, together with government officials, consulting engineers and representatives of private wagon owners. It was probably the biggest crowd the station ever saw.

It was set up in the form of a competition. Road material was unloaded from railway wagons and transferred by lorry to a location a mile away where road repairs were taking place. Two sets of men were taking part, one group using the old shovelling method and one using Smith's Patent Hoppers.

Afterwards the invited guests, though probably not the poor workmen, repaired to the Great Western Hotel at Paddington for luncheon. After lunch Colonel Thwaites of the Smith's Patent Hopper Transport Company gave a speech in which he extolled the device which had been demonstrated as 'an endeavour to eliminate waste – waste of time and waste of wages. It is particularly designed to meet the conditions where under ordinary methods the contents of the wagons have to be transferred by means of men with shovels, an operation which is necessarily slow and which entails long waiting periods for lorries between their journeys.' This would have appealed to the businessmen present – the road contractor would have reduced costs and the railway companies would get more out of their rolling stock. Even the workers would benefit, the Colonel claimed, because their work would be made easier.

Whether the workers actually saw it like that or perhaps recognised the start of the process of creeping mechanisation that would eventually cost them their jobs history does not relate. Certainly this promotional event must have been an unusual interruption in the placid routine of High Street station. I wonder what the railway's employees made of the appearance of so many big-wigs. It would have made for interesting conversations in the pub afterwards!

An idea of the daily routine at this quiet terminus can be gained from the reminiscences of Walter Humphries, published in the Great Western Railway Journal in 1994. Back in 1939

Walter was a porter at the terminus and recalled that the first train of the day arrived from Gerrard's Cross at 6.55 am and left again ten minutes later. As with most services by then, it usually carried only two or three passengers.

This was followed by the branch goods train whose engine was then employed shunting in the goods yard. As only one engine in steam was allowed on the branch at a time, the engine often had to return to the junction before the job was completed so that the next passenger train could come down the branch. This might happen several times if there was a lot of shunting to be done that day. The brake van of the goods train was left behind in the yard giving the guard plenty of time to fry himself a substantial breakfast! There might even be time for a game of darts in the porters' room – so long as the station master wasn't around.

Goods traffic consisted mainly of coal for local merchants, particularly Charringtons. If, for any reason, the single wagons for some of the smaller merchants did not arrive they had nothing to sell that day. One of these, Coleshills, was a father and son operation, delivering by horse and cart. Sandersons, the locally-based wallpaper and fabric printers, occasionally received a wagon of coal for their boilers.

Most weeks a couple of tank wagons would come down the branch for the Red Lion Garage. The oil was pumped across the yard to their premises at the back of the station site. A nearby sawmill, which had its own siding, kept up a whining sound for much of the day – so perhaps it was not so quiet at the little station after all.

# The end of the line

The sparse passenger service from Uxbridge (High Street) to Denham and Gerrard's Cross never amounted to much. The suburban development along its route that the GWR was hoping for just did not happen. Residents of Uxbridge wishing to travel to London had more direct routes from the Metropolitan or from Vine Street. Those who liked their travelling to be really exciting could bounce along on the top of a bumpy tram for the two-hour trip all the way to Holborn via Shepherd's Bush.

The Great Western soon decided that the link to Vine Street would never be worth building. In 1913 traffic receipts from High Street station amounted to a measly £847 for the year, compared with £19,120 from Vine Street and £13,933 from the GWR station at Staines.

The passenger service was withdrawn as a wartime economy in 1917. The line was reduced to a single track when the Army requisitioned the other line. The rails and sleepers were shipped to the Continent for use on the Western Front although it is alleged that the consignment was lost at sea en route. If the rails did make it to France they must have experienced very different conditions from those which had prevailed in the sleepy pre-war valley of the Colne!

Trains were restored in 1920 (weekdays only) but the passenger service was withdrawn once more on 31st August 1939, never to run again. It had hardly been one of the Great Western's more successful branch lines. After that goods trains ran 'when required' until July 1964 and the section between Denham West Junction and the oil depot remained in use until November 1965. The last passenger-carrying train to use Uxbridge (High Street) station was an old GWR diesel railcar operating an enthusiasts' special in September 1954.

# Following the route of the High Street branch

Uxbridge (High Street) station is long gone. The site is now occupied by the futuristic Lincoln building, one of many new office blocks that give parts of the centre of Uxbridge the air of downtown Manhattan. By contrast, opposite the Lincoln building stands the old Treaty House, now the Crown & Treaty Inn. It was here in 1646 that three weeks of discussions took place between representatives of King Charles I and Parliament in an abortive attempt to bring about an end to the Civil War.

The Crown & Treaty is a suitable starting point for an exploration of what is left of the railway as it heads out of Middlesex towards the junction with what is now the Chiltern Line near Denham. The railway track is inaccessible and obliterated by the new development but a pleasant alternative is the towpath of the Grand Union Canal northwards from Uxbridge Lock. Once beyond the town it follows a direct route through surprisingly peaceful countryside, giving a good idea of what the passenger on the railway half a mile to the east would have seen.

Keeping the canal on your left, follow the towpath to bridge 182, just beyond Denham Lock. Here a path leads away to the right into an area of flooded gravel pits, now part of the Colne Valley Park. This area is known as Denham Quarry. Go straight

*The historic Crown & Treaty pub, Uxbridge. High Street station was on the site now occupied by the futuristic Lincoln building in the background. (Author)*

*'First clear your parking space...' Signs in the undergrowth alongside the Uxbridge High Street trackbed through the Colne Valley Park. (Author)*

on along the path which leads between two attractive lakes. Just past the far shore of the lakes the narrow path is crossed by a broader path which is the track of the old railway, although there is nothing to show now that trains ever ran here.

The former trackbed can be followed from here in either direction but is not shown on maps of the Colne Valley Park as a public right of way. To the left it runs northwards on a ridge between two lakes through tall vegetation for about half a mile until your way is blocked by the rusty gates of a gravel works that is still functioning. This, I think, is close to the site of the former triangular junction with the main line.

Southwards the path soon becomes narrower, serving only as access to the platforms on the fishing lakes. On the edges of all these lakes are notices proclaiming the territorial claims of various fishing clubs, which somehow belie the image of anglers as peaceful men. The intrepid explorer, after pushing through the undergrowth for about ten minutes, is rewarded by the sight of the only physical evidence of the railway that I could find, the dark brick parapets of the bridge over the Fray's River, one of the complex network of streams that meander over these flat meadows on the borders of Middlesex and Buckinghamshire. There is a gate here that marks the limit of the fishing club's property. Beyond this the path leads back towards the M40 flyover and Uxbridge.

However, I preferred to retrace my steps to the canal near Denham Lock. I must have looked weary after my explorations because I was hailed by a passing boatman and was offered a lift back to Uxbridge. He introduced himself as Paul Fox, a member of the 1970s rock band The Ruts, who now lives on this stretch of the Grand Union. Our journey turned into some sort of Royal Progress as he greeted various members of the canal community whose narrow-boat homes are moored along the towpath. A hundred years ago who would have forecast that the slow old canal would outlive the bright new railway?

# The stronger sibling

The Vine Street route was always by far the stronger sibling. Industrial and housing development along its route generated an encouraging amount of traffic. By 1938 there were 46 trains each way daily, 17 of which ran through to London, a service that was more comfortable and marginally quicker than the London Transport service. There were even two trains each way daily between Vine Street and Liverpool Street.

In 1958 diesel railcars replaced the steam service. This seemed to herald a new era of improved service but it was not always that simple. The transport writer Chris Leigh recalled how 'at West Drayton the single branch platform on the north side of the line served both the branches to Staines West and Uxbridge. Here would wait identical railcars, one for each destination, a practice which caused perpetual confusion and not a few wasted journeys down the wrong line.'

But in July 1962 the service was reduced to peak hours only. Cynics predicted that this was just the prelude to complete closure and so it proved on 8th September 1962. British Railways (Western Region) was recommended to retain 'the necessary lines and facilities in order that consideration should be given at the appropriate time to the reintroduction of a passenger service to serve Brunel College on its new site at Cowley.' The Western Region management was not impressed by this idea and claimed that the number of students expected at the planned campus would make no difference to the financial viability of the line.

Nothing was done about this plan but it is ironic, in view of Brunel's curt dismissal in 1854 of the notion of Cowley being worthy of a station, that an institution named after him, and based right beside the line at Cowley, might have been the thing to keep one of his lines open. If it had survived another decade or so, how valuable a railway service direct to London would have been for hardworking students wishing to sample the delights of the West End in the evening.

After the passenger service had been withdrawn the line was singled. Goods and parcels traffic lasted until 1964 and trains

*Footbridges to houses in Whitehall Road, Uxbridge. The houses are on the side of the former cutting of the Vine Street branch. (Author)*

also continued to work when required to a new oil and chemicals siding between Cowley and West Drayton.

As with Uxbridge's other lost line, the site of the High Street terminus is now a new office development. It stood near the junction with Cricket Field Road. The modern Hillingdon Road dual-carriageway curves across the old railway route and to find the course of the line it is necessary to negotiate the pedestrian subway to reach Whitehall Road. The railway ran immediately to the east of this road and its course is clearly marked by a strip of new houses which runs all the way to the junction with The Greenway. Opposite the Cowley Brick pub, whose unusual name recalls a once-important local industry, the houses stand at the top of the former cutting with their garages at the level of the trackbed. Southwards the line ran alongside Cleveland Road across the front of Brunel University. The remains of the cutting can best be seen, especially in winter, from the footpath that leads to the university campus from Station Road.

The name Station Road refers to Cowley station but there is nothing to be seen of this as the site has been redeveloped for another linear housing development, which stretches all the way to Peachy Lane. The children I saw playing safely in these cul-de-sacs probably have no idea that trains used to run where they now ride their bicycles! Nearby is the historic St Laurence's church at Cowley, an amazing survival of a tiny rural-looking medieval church.

It is very difficult to see the route of the railway southwards from Cowley into West Drayton. It crossed the main Uxbridge road near the junction with Moorfield Road and bridged the canal just south of its junction with the Slough Arm. Nearby is the Paddington Packet Boat Inn whose name recalls the fast canal boats to London which were one of the wonders of the modern age of transport around 1800.

The single track that curves past Tavistock Road represents the shared start of the Vine Street and Staines West branches. One wonders how far along this section it was that errant passengers realised that they were on the wrong train!

# Uxbridge's Metropolitan memories

At least you can still get to Uxbridge by train, although it is ironic that the last station to be opened in the town, the London Transport one, is the one that survived. The present London Transport station was opened in 1938 but it replaced the original Metropolitan Railway terminus which was nearby in Belmont Road.

That station opened in 1904 and was laid out as a through station, reflecting the original plans to extend the line to High Wycombe via Denham, or even southwards to Windsor. This never happened and, because it was not very convenient for the town centre, it was replaced by the present station. In its heyday, however, the refreshment room at the Belmont Road terminus was, it seems, well known for its cleanliness, belying the reputation of railway refreshment rooms across the country. A

Mr & Mrs Moss ran it and their home-cooked ham rolls were renowned the length of the line. In winter Mr Moss made sure that the room's welcoming coal fire was kept burning at all times!

Not all the staff at Belmont Road were as conscientious. When the Piccadilly Line services were extended to Uxbridge from South Harrow the local paper reported that the new service was advertised merely by a scruffy and badly-hung canvas sign.

The Metropolitan seemed to have been rather churlish towards competing railway companies that wanted to use its station. There were just two platforms. The main buildings were on the southern platform, which was just a shade nearer the town centre. This platform was reserved for the Metropolitan's own trains. Those of the District Railway and later the Piccadilly Line were relegated to the other platform, which had virtually no covering and was accessible only by an unsheltered path behind the buffer stops.

After closure, the Belmont Road terminus was used for a number of years as a warehouse. In the 1950s it was derelict and being used for storage by a local greengrocer who piled orange boxes along the length of the platform. Wholesale grocers, Alfred

*Piccadilly and District Line trains at Uxbridge (Belmont Road). (Hillingdon Library Services)*

Button & Sons, had since 1913 leased buildings in the goods yard. They received favourable terms on condition that the Metropolitan Railway would get a certain level of traffic from the company.

In 1926 the wholesalers wanted to extend their operations at the old station but sent most of their traffic by road rather than rail. The railway company insisted that Buttons withdrew all but one of the lorries that had been used between Uxbridge and the London Docks and send the bulk of their goods by rail. This is what happened, much of it going through the Met's Farringdon goods depot.

This arrangement continued until reconstruction of Uxbridge station by the London Passenger Transport Board in 1939 led to the closure of the old yard. The site has now been redeveloped and nothing remains of the original terminus, although the observant traveller looking out on the right-hand side of the train as it draws into Uxbridge station today may be able to work out where it was.

Just down the line, Hillingdon station replaces the original station opened by the Metropolitan Railway in 1923 as a halt to serve the new 'Metroland' housing developments in the area. It was a very basic timber structure reached from the western side of Long Lane and soon the well-heeled customers were complaining about the open-fronted platform shelters which gave them little protection from the elements. Improvements were made in 1931 and the station was renamed Hillingdon (Swakeleys) after the local grand mansion. The station was resited westwards in June 1992, made necessary by the widening of the adjoining A40 Western Avenue. For a few months the platforms of the old station served as pedestrian access to the new one but soon afterwards the original Hillingdon station was demolished.

# 3
# Kempton And Feltham Memories

*Kempton Park Pumping Station to Hampton
Waterworks
Kempton Park station
Red flags and freight at Feltham*

*Victorian steam engine houses at Hampton Waterworks. The Water Board
railway ran behind these buildings. View looking towards Sunbury. (Author)*

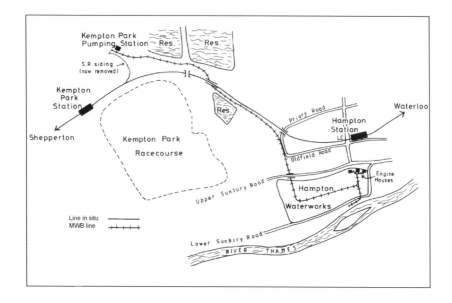

# Kempton Park Pumping Station to Hampton Waterworks

Between Hampton and Sunbury stations the suburban line from Waterloo to Shepperton curves northwards to avoid the ancient Royal Manor of Kempton. The pleasure ground of kings in medieval times, it is now best known for its racecourse, home to the famous Boxing Day meeting.

To engineers, however, the name of Kempton is associated with the Metropolitan Water Board and its pumping station whose magnificent engines are being painstakingly restored to working order by the Kempton Great Engines Trust. A network of reservoirs was established alongside the river here after 1852 when the Metropolis Water Act prohibited the abstraction of Thames water below Teddington Lock. In 1902 these came under the control of the MWB whose programme of improvements included the building of a 2 ft gauge railway between the works at Kempton Park and Hampton, with a branch to their

46

waterfront wharf and coal-bunkers. The line was opened in 1915 and operated for just over twenty years before the new works with steam turbines and coal conveyers was opened, making the railway redundant.

Before then coal supplies for the waterworks had been shipped by Thames barge upriver to the wharf, which lay south of the filter beds by the Lower Sunbury Road, between the road and the river and opposite Platts Ait. As much as 110 tons was consumed daily by the massive pumping engines and this was a daunting load to shift by horse and cart up from the waterfront. It was not too bad to transport the tonnage needed by the works at Hampton but it was a long uphill trudge to Kempton. The roads in the area were not in a condition to cope with this heavy traffic. Even the main roads in Sunbury did not get their first tarmacadam surface until about 1915 – hence the need for the railway.

Once the new line opened, coal unloaded from the barges was transferred by a high-level travelling crane into a large hopper at the water's edge and then transferred by rail to the pumping houses. From the wharf the line crossed the Lower Sunbury Road by a level crossing equipped with gates. The narrow gauge track then curved between the filter beds, with a short branch linking to the engine house of the former Southwark and Vauxhall Water Works, south of the Upper Sunbury Road, by its junction with Percy Road, Hampton.

The track then curved sharply north to run under the Upper Sunbury Road (which was carried on a steel girder bridge lined with concrete) and northwards, past the end of Oldfield Road, towards what was in those days the Southern Railway's Shepperton branch. It ran parallel to the standard gauge track past a small reservoir and the Engine House of the former Grand Junction Water Works, before diving under the 'main line' and heading for the pumping station a short distance to the north-west. The railway here climbed up a fairly steep gradient and curved round close to the embankment of the reservoir before crossing Kempton Park Lane by another level crossing, again protected by gates.

The line continued westwards and came to its northern terminus between the old (1906) pumping station of the

Kempton Park Works and a standard gauge branch from the Southern Railway at Kempton Park station. This siding had been constructed so that at times when the river was made unnavigable by floods or when the Thames lightermen were on strike, the coal could be brought in on the Southern Railway line and unloaded at Kempton Park. At the end of this short branch there was an embankment and hoppers into which the coal from the standard gauge wagons could be deposited.

Operations ceased around the start of the Second World War and the railway has been completely dismantled. Most of the route is on Water Board land and fears of terrorist attacks on water supply installations ensure that these areas are securely fenced and inaccessible. Back in 1992 Ken Heselton, a noted local historian, was able to explore what remained and described what he saw in a publication of the Sunbury & Shepperton Local History Society. This included a stretch of embankment south of the Lower Sunbury Road, between the road and the water's edge.

Old maps show the railway alongside Kempton Road, which ran along the western edge of Hampton Waterworks, connecting the Lower and Upper Sunbury Roads. Kempton Road is no more, closed off by high metal fencing. The nearest you can get is to follow the London Cycle Way path that runs parallel to the old road, a few hundred yards to the west. Red notices warn that the path is under surveillance – what the security guards would make of anyone scrambling up the bank on the left to try to photograph the old line of the railway from east to west across the waterworks is anybody's guess. Once the Upper Sunbury Road is reached, turn right and follow this road for a short distance towards Hampton. The light-controlled crossing for the Cycle Way is right by the fenced-off end of the former Kempton Road. You can just catch a glimpse of the bridge, still in place, which carried the main road across the railway but the line's route northwards is inaccessible.

Following the main road into Hampton takes you away from the line but it is worth it to see the impressive range of Victorian pumping houses and associated waterworks buildings.

To rejoin the water board railway from Hampton village, it is necessary to follow Oldfield Road from the level crossing at

*Water company clock tower in Hampton village. (Author)*

Hampton station – a station which somehow manages to retain a country-railway atmosphere. Oldfield Road turns sharply right at the end and from here runs alongside the track of the narrow gauge line. Its route can still be traced in a shallow overgrown cutting behind the ubiquitous metal fencing. At a point near the Shepperton line bridge over Oldfield Road, the little railway curved away to the left on what is now inaccessible Thames Water land, to run alongside the 'main line'.

Where the narrow gauge line came alongside the Shepperton branch the Water Board stored water pipes. These pipes were stacked on lengths of the old rail. A few short sections of track survived in situ and were seen by Mr Heselton in 1992. The course of the line can be easily seen from Shepperton branch trains for some distance on either side of the point where the Water Board line passed underneath them. The rails were then still in place at the Kempton Park Lane crossing, embedded in the road surface, but I was not able to see for myself whether they still remain.

The Kempton Great Engines Trust have long-term plans to open to the public. When they do so it might be possible to see what little now remains of the railway's terminus.

Sadly nothing is left of the three tank engines built for the line by Kerr, Stuart & Company of Stoke on Trent. Named, somewhat unimaginatively, *Sunbury*, *Kempton* and *Hampton*, they were noted for their attractive design, smart green paint-work and gleaming brass domes. What a sight they would make racing the utilitarian suburban electric units on their parallel tracks through Kempton's woodland!

# Kempton Park station

Kempton Park station is not on a 'Lost Railway' and is still open to passengers on race days only – but one train service to the station, still perhaps recalled but certainly unlamented by its unwilling users, has long since gone – the POW specials of the Second World War.

Towards the end of the war Kempton Park racecourse was

50

*German POWs arriving under guard at Kempton Park. (Sunbury and Shepperton Local History Society)*

used as a Reception Centre for German and Italian prisoners. They arrived there in their thousands, especially after the North African campaign and the Allied invasion of Europe. There they were, in the delicate wording of the time, 'decontaminated' and interrogated before being dispersed to camps elsewhere.

Kempton Park station is unusual in that there is no public access from it, except to the racecourse itself. This made it an ideal secure location. The trains that brought the prisoners were made up of corridor coaches that had fewer doors than the old suburban stock that formed the normal trains on the Shepperton line. This meant that fewer guards were needed to foil escape attempts.

Once they arrived the prisoners were accommodated wherever there was space while the British troops guarding them occupied huts on the Paddock and alongside Park Road. It was a familiar sight for local people to see the prisoners being exercised, marching from Kempton along the Staines Road as

51

far as the Spelthorne pub at Ashford Common where, tantalisingly for the thirsty men no doubt, they stopped, turned and were marched back again. Some were put to work in market gardens where one group, working for the aptly-named Mr George Roote, unbeknown to their employer once carved swastikas on a consignment of swedes destined for an RAF camp!

The course remained in the hands of the military until September 1946 and did not reopen for racing until Easter 1947. The 1950s were the heyday of Race Day specials from Waterloo to Kempton Park. After they had disgorged the eager punters the trains were parked end-to-end all the way from Sunbury station to Shepperton to be called forward one by one to return the poorer but wiser racegoers to London after the last race.

A 'lost' line, lost in the sense that it was never even built, was the proposed extension of the Shepperton line across the Thames to Chertsey. Shepperton station was built as a through station rather than a terminus but work on the extension never even started. In April 1982 an early morning arrival from Waterloo attempted to get to Chertsey by failing to stop at the end of the line. It ended up dramatically poised over the pavement at the end of Shepperton High Street. Luckily the train was virtually empty and nobody was hurt.

# Red flags and freight at Feltham

Feltham station between Richmond and Staines was once touted as the starting point of a direct rail link to Heathrow Airport. That plan seems to have been shelved in favour of the Piccadilly Line extension and the Heathrow Express service from Paddington. Today it is just another stop – albeit an important one on the main line from Waterloo to Reading – but it was once the location of one of London's most important freight marshalling yards, built by the London & South Western Railway in 1921-2. There were still Prisoners of War at the time and they were employed on the construction work.

The yard, the second largest in the country, was situated between the station and the triangular junction with the Hounslow loop at a point where the tracks crossed the River Crane on the southern edge of Hounslow Heath – an area infamous in the past as the haunt of highwaymen! The river posed something of a problem and a tunnel culvert was constructed under the tracks to cope with the river's flow at times of flood. It still exists but securely barred to foolhardy, if intrepid, explorers.

Feltham Yard came into its own during the Second World War when its use enabled goods traffic to avoid London. It was still a major centre of operations in the 1950s and early '60s but as general wagon traffic declined rapidly it proved surplus to requirements and was closed in September 1968. Its most prominent feature was the main control building with its clock tower. This survived as a derelict shell until it was demolished in the mid 1990s. There are still some concrete buildings on the site today, as well as a number of subways that once provided safe staff access under the lines.

As in other parts of Middlesex, the coming of the railway opened up a region that had for centuries been largely agricultural. Strange as it may seem to those who know the area now, it was desirable commuter country for turn-of-the-century middle-class breadwinners who could afford a house in the leafy countryside around Feltham and Bedfont whence they could travel daily to Waterloo. Lines of suburban dwellings sprang up on the sites of market gardens and orchards as the villages expanded.

The only industry in the area before that time had been the gunpowder mills on the rivers flowing across the heath. Perhaps their dangerous proximity contributed to the lack of houses in the vicinity! In 1914 the Army took over the historic Feltham House and some of its grounds, including part of Hanworth Park, and established a depot for the Royal Army Service Corps.

To serve this complex a branch from a point on the main line just west of Feltham station was built. It curved away southwards and into a small cutting, passing by a chemical works and through an area of open ground known as High Fields. It crossed Feltham High Street just where Barclay's Bank now stands.

There was a large level-crossing gate across the railway on the north side of the High Street which was opened when a train was ready to take goods into the Army depot. A man with a red flag would saunter to the centre of the road to warn the traffic to stop. The little engine with its load of trucks would then pass over the road and into Browells Lane, passing the old Red Lion pub with its horse trough outside.

The large gates in the perimeter fence of the depot were on the site of the original entrance and drive to Feltham House, which the railway followed. The line continued in use until 1958 and the rails remained in place until the centre of Feltham was redeveloped in the 1960s. They were quite a hazard to cyclists and over the years many unfortunates came to grief along Browells Lane turning into the High Street when they accidentally caught their front wheel in the gap by the rail!

# 4

# Brunel's Last Line

## *Southall to Brentford Dock*

*Southall station, c1910. (Ealing Library and Information Service)*

Brentford Dock is now an upmarket housing and marina complex but in its day it was one of West London's most significant transport interchanges where goods brought in from the Great Western Railway were transhipped onto river or canal barge. The branch line from Southall which served it has the distinction of being the last line planned and executed by the great Isambard Kingdom Brunel.

The Great Western Railway in the 1840s found itself denied adequate links to the canal and river navigation systems that were still of crucial importance. A contemporary writer claimed that 'the possession of Brentford is as vital to the Great Western Railway as the possession of Sebastapol to the Allies'!

The company had the rather lukewarm patriotic support of the

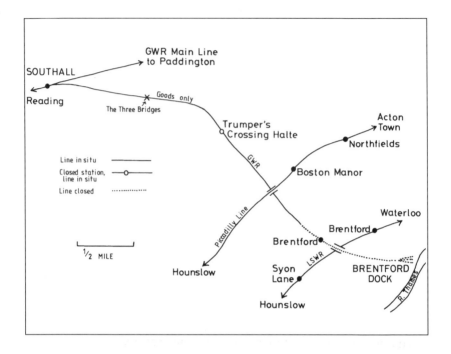

Duke of Northumberland at nearby Syon House for it was stated that 'His Grace, although not desirous of having a railway so close to Syon land, with his accustomed liberality, sacrificed his private feelings to the advantage of the neighbourhood and allowed the line to pass without opposition.'

Various schemes were proposed but it was not until August 1855 that the Great Western & Brentford Railway Bill was approved by Parliament, despite opposition from the Grand Union Canal Company and also the London & South Western Railway, which already had a station at Brentford on its Hounslow Loop Line. Clauses were put into the Act of Parliament to protect these parties. The aqueduct at Hanwell, where the railway was to pass under the canal, was to be built, with the canal being diverted into a temporary channel during construction. The railway was to be liable to a penalty of £10 per hour for any time that the passage of boats was made impossible. The exact specification of the bridge over the London & South

Western Railway's line had to be approved by that company's engineer.

Brunel was a busy man at the height of his powers but his various maritime enterprises were occupying more and more of his time. Perhaps he did not give the Brentford project his full attention. For whatever reason, he seriously underestimated the cost of constructing the dock at Brentford and further capital had to be raised under two more Acts of Parliament in 1857 and 1859. The line was officially opened on 15th July 1859, a month and a half later than planned, but even then the approach road to the dock from Brentford High Street had not been completed.

Things apparently did not go entirely to plan. The railway officials and distinguished guests travelled upstream from London on two paddle steamers specially chartered for the occasion. On each vessel was a brass band primed to salute the approach to Brentford Dock with a rousing rendition of 'See The Conquering Hero Comes'. Unfortunately, witnesses reported, the bands were not quite in time with each other and the branch got off to a somewhat discordant start.

The official account of the opening ceremony stated that 'those travelling were struck not more with the scenery which the line traverses' (which included the much-admired distant prospect of the Hanwell Lunatic Asylum) 'than by the permanence and solidity which characterise the construction.' The day's proceedings ended with what was described as 'a repast of the most recherché description'. This apparently involved speeches and toasts in honour of almost everybody except of course the demon LSWR whose traffic the new railway was hoping to steal. Speakers outlined visions of the 'tasteful detached villas' whose construction would inevitably follow the opening of the railway.

It all went on rather late. The VIPs departed fairly early on the special train back to Paddington. Some of the other guests, a little the worse for wear perhaps, had no choice but to accept the services of the hated rival line to get them home.

The dock complex eventually contained six large warehouses, a wharf on the riverfront, a quay and the dock itself, which had a covered basin at the west end. There was a goods transfer shed designed by Brunel but this was destroyed by fire in 1920. Vessels of up to 300 tons could enter the dock from the Thames.

Forty-ton hydraulic cranes were installed in 1919 and two electrically-operated travelling cranes in 1932.

Freight was the Brentford branch's raison d'être; the passenger service was very much an afterthought, not starting until May the following year. Plans for an extension to a riverside terminus and a ferry link to Kew Gardens were considered but abandoned as too expensive. Nothing came either of a proposed extension across the river to Twickenham – scuppered by opposition from the LSWR.

The station, on the north side of Brentford High Street, well short of the dock itself, was basic and unimpressive. Its opening in September 1859 was delayed because the Board of Trade inspector insisted on the provision of 'a handrail over the top of the outside girder of the overbridge to prevent passengers from getting out in the dark and falling over into the road'. The station eventually opened without ceremony in May 1860 but by 1866 there were complaints that the exposed wooden staircase from the street to the platforms was 'unsuitable for ladies in rainy or windy weather'. The mind boggles.

Originally there had been a single line laid to Brunel's 7 ft broad gauge but in 1861 a mixed gauge (broad and standard) track was built alongside it exclusively for freight trains while the passenger service ran on the broad gauge. Normal double-line working only happened after the broad gauge track was converted to standard gauge in 1875.

At the Southall end the junction faced away from London. This reflected the original idea of the promoters – to provide freight trains from the west or Midlands with a direct route to the wharves on the Thames – but this was hardly conducive to stimulating any commuter traffic into Paddington. In any case the LSWR service into Waterloo was far more convenient. To placate the influential Earl of Jersey, owner of Osterley Park, the GWR line ran due almost due east from Southall and only later turned south-east towards the river.

Near the change in direction was the most interesting feature of the line, Windmill Bridge or the Three Bridges, where the road passed over the canal and the railway ran underneath both in a three-decker arrangement. The railway ran in a cutting at this point but then emerged into the valley of the little River Brent. In

*The Three Bridges: view from track level. (Ealing Library and Information Service)*

1883 the Brentford branch was crossed on a viaduct by the new Metropolitan District Railway line to Hounslow. In 1925 the Great West Road was constructed north of Brentford High Street and an impressive girder bridge was provided to carry the railway over it. This remained a prominent landmark until this section of the line was closed in 1965. Just north of Brentford station the branch crossed the LSWR line to Hounslow which had been opened in 1849.

The Great Western tried various measures to stimulate the passenger revenues, which remained stubbornly disappointing. Steam railcars were experimented with from 1904 and on 1st July of that year an intermediate station was opened. 'Station' is rather too grand a word though. The quaintly-named Trumper's Crossing (for Osterley Park) Halte (the 'e' apparently was due to the fact that the steam railcar concept had originated in France) was intended to bring in passengers from the expanding suburb of Hanwell, a quarter of a mile to the east, but the primitive platforms with very basic shelters sat half a mile away on the other side of the canal – hardly an attractive prospect on a dark night when there was a warm tram at the end of your road. Whatever traffic potential it may have had was soon crushed by the opening of the electric tramway along Boston Road between Brentford and Hanwell in 1906. It is unlikely that Osterley Park, optimistically included in the halt's grandiose title, ever generated significant numbers of passengers. The name is a bit of a puzzle anyway, the Trumper family from the nearby Warren Farm had strongly objected to the line being built in the first place!

It was no surprise when the passenger service was withdrawn in March 1915 as part of the GWR's wartime economies. It was perhaps more of one when it was restored in 1920. From 1929 it was restricted to peak hours only and by this time the halt, despite its name change to 'Trumper's Crossing for South Hanwell and Osterley Park', had been closed and demolished in 1926. Apparently the typical GWR pagoda-roofed corrugated iron huts that had graced its platforms were transported to South Greenford Halt on the West Ealing to Greenford line where they remained in use until the 1970s.

Services were suspended again in 1942 and never resumed.

*Front-coupled tank locomotive no 1165 with trailer car at Trumper's Crossing Halte before 1920. (Chiswick Library)*

The appearance of little diesel railcars on the line in 1951 was a false dawn – they were manufactured by Associated Commercial Vehicles at Southall and were simply being tested before being sent to work on lines elsewhere where there was somewhat more potential. The station at Brentford was finally pulled down in 1957 but the overgrown platforms remained well into the 1990s. As no housing development ever took place along the branch, it is surprising that the passenger service lasted as long as 82 years.

The industrial development along the Great West Road, however, continued to stimulate an encouraging amount of freight business. A new Brentford Town goods yard was opened on the north side of the new road in 1930. Private sidings were provided for biscuit manufacturers MacFarlane, Lang & Company and the Firestone Tyre and Rubber Company. There were two 6 ton cranes and access to the Grand Union Canal. Even in the 1950s a wide range of goods and materials was being transported. A regular business in the 1950s was the shipment of Morris cars brought down by rail from Oxford. However, in the 1960s reductions in the use of coal, the new strategy of 'containerisation' for which the by-now antiquated facilities at Brentford Dock were not suitable and the switch to road transport, coupled with the poor road access from Brentford High Street, all conspired to make the line become uneconomic. Most of the traffic had had to be transhipped again when it reached London Docks, which made no business sense any more. Brentford Dock closed at the end of 1964 and the last part of the branch, together with the bridge over the Great West Road, was dismantled.

However, Brentford Town yard remained in use until 1970 and most of the rest of the line from Southall remained active. There were private industrial sidings south of the Piccadilly Line bridge and these handled quantities of stone and aggregate. In 1977 the Greater London Council began a scheme that involved

*The Brentford branch is still in use for freight traffic for most of its length. Looking towards Brentford from the site of Trumper's Crossing Halte. (Author)*

large quantities of refuse from the capital being shipped out from a new West London Refuse Transfer Station (north of the old Brentford Town yard) to landfill sites in Bedfordshire and Oxfordshire. A 30-year contract was signed resulting in six trains per week. Each train had 20 wagons and the total load per train was 800 tons. 'Where there's muck there's brass' – on such unglamorous business Brunel's last line continued to fulfil a worthwhile function.

Much of the line then remains open for this traffic. From Southall – location of a steam preservation centre – the single track still leads away south-eastwards, skirting the edge of Osterley Park. The fact that the line is still used by freight trains, albeit infrequently, means that the track is securely fenced. Anyone trespassing on the line would face a very heavy fine. This is, of course, absolutely right but somewhat frustrating at the Three Bridges, where the best view of this unique three-level, three-transport mode crossing would probably be obtained from track level. However, a good impression can be obtained from

*Remains of the old viaduct, The Ham, near Brentford Dock. (Author)*

*The Three Bridges: road, canal and railway. (Ealing Library and Information Service)*

the canal towpath on the middle level or from Windmill Lane, which runs across the top. Across the railway track there are the remains of a two-arched bridge at a slightly lower level. This acted as buttresses for the cutting sides' retaining walls. The canal aqueduct was constructed from 140 tons of cast iron forming a trough 8ft deep.

From the Three Bridges the canal towpath past the Hanwell flight of locks offers an interesting and mostly attractive walk of about three miles to Brentford. There is a welcoming pub, the Fox, reached by turning down a path near the bottom lock – a good place for a leisurely lunch. About a quarter of a mile further on Trumper's Way provides access off Boston Road to an industrial estate and the canal towpath walk. A little way past the bridge over the canal the road bends sharply to the left and a gated footpath leads across the railway line and on to Windmill Lane and Osterley Park. This is a good place to get close to the line but trains do still run and the safety notices must be observed. This is the site of the short-lived Trumper's Crossing Halte of which nothing visible remains.

South of this point the line is less easily accessible as it passes under the motorway and on past Wyke Green golf course to its present end in the industrial area. Heavy lorries make Transport Avenue, leading to the Great West Road, an unpleasant and dangerous place for pedestrians and it is best avoided. It is far better to follow the towpath to Brentford Locks – an interesting industrial archaeology excursion in itself.

The 21st century intrudes as the canal walk passes under the Great West Road on the approach to Brentford. Commercial buildings of elegant futuristic design appear on both sides of the canal and smartly-dressed young trainee managers pace the towpath speaking urgently into their mobile phones. This is the brave new world of the Brentford Executive Centre but in the past it was where the Brentford Town Goods Depot was opened (in 1930). The massive girder bridge that was built to carry the branch across the new road in 1925 was demolished in 1965.

The landscape becomes more down-at-heel once the bridge bearing South West Trains' Hounslow Loop has been passed and the locks of Brentford appear amid more building sites. This was the location of the passenger terminus and a few of the arches

*The railway bridge at The Ham, 1958. (John Gillham)*

that supported it remain, now used by more of the ubiquitous car-repair firms. The base of the signal box can also be seen next to the bridge abutment. Immediately across the road the viaduct has been demolished completely but from the bridge some more arches can be seen on the far side of the canal. These are in The Ham, a narrow road that led, inadequately, to Brentford Dock and the end of the line.

Where the rest of the old trackbed has disappeared to is a bit of a mystery until you see road traffic crossing what is obviously an old railway bridge a few bends further along The Ham. This is Augustus Close, built along the rest of the rail route to give access to the modern Brentford Dock housing estate. All the blocks have Latin names, in tribute to the legend that Julius Caesar led his invading Roman troops across the river here. In the car parking area behind Nero Court, of all places, the last traces of the Brentford branch can be seen – a few low arches in a wall that must have marked the boundary of the goods yard.

# 5
# Lines Around South Acton

*A silly way to get to Hammersmith*
*'The Tea Run'*
*Old Kew Junction*

*Vincent Road, Acton. South Acton District Railway station at top left with the North London station beyond. (Ealing Library and Information Service)*

## A silly way to get to Hammersmith

The railways with the most imposing titles are often the least significant. The grandiose-sounding North & South West Junction line, for example, comprised nothing more than the few miles from Kew Bridge to Willesden Junction via Acton,

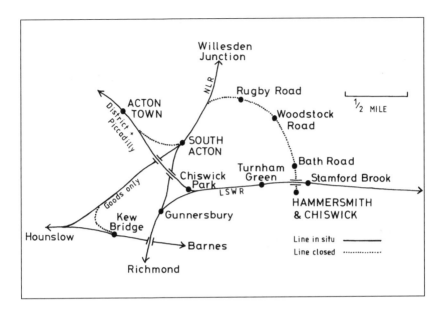

most of which eventually became part of the North London line and which still operates to this day.

Willesden Junction station, opened in 1866, was a most confusing place from which to begin a journey. Trains started at alternate quarter hours from the separate High Level platforms of the lines to Kew and Kensington. It was alleged that the station was haunted by the ghosts of passengers still trying to find their way out, and a more logical rebuilding didn't take place until 1894.

The really pointless section of the complex network in this part of West London though was the one and a half mile branch from vaguely near Acton to a station known as Hammersmith & Chiswick, which was in reality not in either place. Curving slowly through 180 degrees it looped from its terminus back to a junction on the 'main' line, pointing in a direction that no-one wanted to go!

It seemed an oddly hopeless enterprise. If extended a little farther to the river it could have had a wharf that realised some revenue but no plans to construct such an extension were ever considered.

Freight traffic began on 1st May 1857 and passengers were first carried over a year later, on 8th April 1858, by which time the N&SWJR had managed to acquire an engine, having earlier considered horse power! A little saddle tank chuffed with one coach along the line nine times a day to and from Acton Gatehouse Junction where North London Railway trains stopped to pick up the coach. Returning NLR trains merely slowed down briefly while the coupling to the branch coach was detached by the guard. Derailments caused by this illegal procedure were apparently frequent.

As at Staines West (Chapter 1) the terminus was a converted private house on the main road. The passenger walked in, purchased his ticket in the hall and continued out into the back garden where he had his first sight of the little train that was to be the first stage in a circuitous journey.

From 1865 the trains from the branch ran through to Acton (now Acton Central) after reversing at Gatehouse Junction, ending the dangerous Heath Robinson antics endured previously. From 1880 a new interchange station called South Acton

*A single-coach train leaves South Acton station on the shuttle service to Acton Town on the last day of service, 28th February 1959. (John H. Meredith)*

70

was provided with a separate bay platform where N&SWJR Hammersmith & Chiswick trains could terminate with greater dignity and their few passengers connect with the North London service.

By now Hammersmith was growing into a populous suburb but this growth was almost entirely due to the direct services offered by the Hammersmith & City Railway to Paddington and Aldgate from 1864 and the Metropolitan District Railway from 1874. There was, however, now quite a significant freight traffic serving coalyards at the terminus, a dyeworks and an asphalt plant.

When the London & North Western Railway took over the North London in 1909 they introduced a one-class 48-seat steam railmotor which became affectionately known as 'Little Jenny' and which provided a half-hour service. As a further economy tickets were sold by a conductor-guard, anticipating more recent practice on underused branches, but the range of destinations available was very limited and passengers were faced with the inconvenience of having to rebook at South Acton for most destinations. Very basic timber halts were opened at Rugby Road, Woodstock Road and Bath Road in an attempt to attract more passengers.

It was too little too late. The opening in 1912 of the nearby Stamford Brook station on the Metropolitan District Line, which crossed the branch near its terminus, killed off what traffic there was and, under wartime economies, the passenger services ceased at the end of December 1916, unmourned by most and never to return. The terminus became a shop and a private house once more but a daily goods train continued to make its way down what had become a mere siding until the 1950s. There was a ten mile per hour speed limit and the train crew had to stop the train to open the level crossing gates at Bath Road themselves.

In 1956 an enthusiasts' excursion brought four packed coaches down the line to Hammersmith & Chiswick – possibly more passengers in one day than in its entire previous existence. The last goods train inched its way along the track in May 1965.

For many years after that passengers on the District Line trains rumbling over the viaduct between Turnham Green and Stamford Brook could see the overgrown yard of this curious little terminus but in the 1990s the site was finally earmarked for housing. It is now a residential development called Ravensmede Way. From here you can see the iron bridge breaking up the brick viaduct carrying the District and Piccadilly trains. This was where the branch passed underneath. With the eye of faith the route of the line can still be traced, however, as it loops in almost half a circle around the edges of the exclusive Bedford Park estate. It crossed Stamford Brook Road where the modern Seventh Day Adventist Church (built on the trackbed) now stands and then ran behind the houses in Abinger Road and Greenend Road. There is little to be seen here although the footpath from Woodstock Road to the Evelyn Estate has a suspicious rise in it which may be the remains of a bridge over the line. A little further on near a scout hut there is an overgrown plot of land which must be the old railway.

The line ran along the northern edge of Southfields Recreation Ground but there is no trace of it here or on the approach to the junction with the North London line near South Acton. The only clue is the significant angle of an industrial building near the former junction which suggests that it may have been aligned with the track of the branch.

However, for much of its route the line of the branch still forms the boundary between the postal district of W4 (Chiswick and Bedford Park) where it adjoins W3 (Acton) and W12 (Shepherd's Bush). Now that postcodes are used as a measure for such things as insurance premiums and assessment of credit-worthiness, this could be its most important legacy!

# 'The Tea Run'

South Acton station was also the terminus for one of the more curious outposts of the District Line – the one-coach train that shuttled every twenty minutes or so to and from Acton Town, all of two minutes away.

This curious little service, which was withdrawn in 1959, was a relic of a more ambitious scheme to link the North London line with the Metropolitan District Railway stations westwards to

*An eastbound Piccadilly Line train heading for Wood Green runs into Acton Town station. The South Acton shuttle service departed from the other side of this platform, off the picture to the right. (Stations UK)*

Hounslow and Ealing. Various schemes were put forward to do this after South Acton station was opened in 1880 but it was not until 1899 that the first trains passed over the newly-completed loop line.

At first the new line was only used for goods trains, mainly carrying materials for the Ealing and South Harrow line which was opened in 1903. Passenger services began in June 1905, running between South Acton and Hounslow Barracks (later known as Hounslow West). Connections were made at South Acton with the steam-operated North London line trains to Willesden Junction and Broad Street.

Once a small country village despite its proximity to London, Acton had grown in the 1880s and '90s, becoming a mainly working-class area although some of the older villas and a few market gardens survived. The area southwards towards Turnham Green had a number of laundries and drying-grounds, washing and whitening the garments of middle-class Kensington, and the district became nicknamed 'Soapsud Island'.

73

The plans to run trains from Hounslow or Ealing onto the North London, continuing to Broad Street never came to anything and, as an economy measure during the First World War, the physical connection with the North London tracks was cut, although the possibility of through trains was not finally abandoned until 1934 when the signal box controlling the junction was demolished. In 1913 the service was reduced to just a shuttle between South Acton and Acton Town but after the war trains began running again from South Acton to South Harrow, Uxbridge and Hounslow. Little was done to modernise the District's ramshackle corrugated iron station building at South Acton. There remained the somewhat incongruous situation of two separate sets of steps to two separate booking offices for the District and North London (by now LMS) stations.

It was the extension of the Piccadilly Line westwards over the District Line route from Hammersmith that finally put an end to the loop's usefulness as a through route. Acton Town station was rebuilt in 1932 with just a dead-end platform for the South Acton trains. It was somewhat superfluous to label the service on the ends of the single-coach trains as 'Acton Town Non-Stop' and 'South Acton All Stations', yet this was apparently done! The loop was reduced to a single track and converted for one-man operation. It was the first instance of one-man operation on the London Underground.

The one-coach train, nicknamed 'The Pony', continued to trundle up and down on its two-minute journey for another quarter of a century. It was widely believed that its timetable was related to the time it took the crew to brew up a pot of tea – 'there and back while the kettle boils' – hence its other nickname: 'The Tea Run'.

It must have been well used, though. In the 1950s the train ran every ten minutes and even more frequently in rush hours. Closure was proposed by London Transport in 1958 (when Sunday services were withdrawn) and, despite local opposition, the last train ran on 28th February 1959.

There is little left to see of this idiosyncratic little line but at Acton Town station the bay platform for the South Acton shuttle still remains hidden behind large advertising hoardings. Go up onto the footbridge and look over the side, slightly to the left of

*Demolition of the bridge over Bollo Lane, January 1965. (Ealing Library and Information Service)*

the stairway to platform 4. There is still a staircase down to it but this is closed to the public. Over forty years after closure the platform and its canopy remain but passengers on District or Piccadilly Line trains pausing at the station would have no idea that it is there, the hoardings totally masking the view.

From Acton Town station Gunnersbury Lane and Bollo Lane lead towards South Acton. On the right modern offices and factories hide the old trackbed. One of these buildings is Frank Pick House, named after the man responsible for developing the characteristic London Transport 'house-style' in the 1930s. In 1964 council flats were built on the site of the old embankment (now levelled) between Bollo Lane and South Acton.

The bridge over Bollo Lane, just by the entrance to the former London Transport Acton Works, was dismantled in January 1965, not without incident. It collapsed into the road and the wreckage had to be cut up where it had fallen, blocking the road for several days. On the north side of Bollo Lane the garden centre and Poores DIY store occupy the old trackbed. At South Acton station a nearby recreation ground was extended over the former trackbed, obliterating all traces, apart from a short overgrown section which merges into the allotments.

An episode of the archetypal eighties television series 'Minder' was, I understand, filmed here with the present South Acton station masquerading as 'Acton Green' – one of the few variants on the name of Acton that is not blessed with a station in real life! There is nothing left of the tiny little District Line terminus at South Acton which stood next to the west side of the North London (now Silverlink Metro) platforms, the site being now part of the allotments.

Those who regret the loop's destruction point to the fact that if the North London line had been incorporated into the London Transport network, as was proposed at various times, the loop could have become part of a convenient route between north and east London and Heathrow Airport. Think of the congestion on the roads and on the Piccadilly Line that this might have saved!

# Old Kew Junction

There is another ghost at South Acton. Branching south-westwards off the line to Gunnersbury and Richmond, a freight-only line leads to Old Kew Junction west of Kew Bridge station on the South West Trains Hounslow Loop. This was part of the previously-mentioned North & South Western Junction Railway to Willesden Junction on the LNWR. It was opened for freight in February 1853 and a North London Railway passenger service from Kew to Hampstead Road or Fenchurch Street. In 1854 the NLR began a Hampstead Road to Windsor service via Brentford and Staines which also used this route but this was not encouraged by the LSWR and lasted only a year. A proposed service from Euston to Hounslow or Brentford never happened at all.

Even more obscure was a service introduced in 1858 from Hampstead Road to Twickenham via Acton, Kew, Chiswick, Barnes and Richmond – a procedure which involved reversing the direction of travel at both Kew and Barnes. Quite an operation in those steam-hauled days! The opening in 1869 of the LSWR line from Kensington to Richmond via Shepherd's Bush allowed a direct run from Willesden and Richmond via South Acton and meant that such circuitous operations were no longer needed.

For most of its existence the Old Kew Junction to South Acton link has seen only goods trains. In May 2000 though Anglia Trains began running trains from Basingstoke to destinations in East Anglia routed via Staines, Feltham and the North London line to Stratford. This utilised the Kew–Acton link but was apparently as unsuccessful as the other short-lived experiments that have passed this way. It was withdrawn at the end of September 2002.

# 6
# Around Shepherd's Bush

*Addison Road to Richmond via Hammersmith
Grove
Latimer Road to Shepherd's Bush*

*Shepherd's Bush station, c1949. (Hammersmith and Fulham Archives and
Local History Centre)*

## Addison Road to Richmond via Hammersmith Grove

Alert passengers on District or Piccadilly Line trains approaching
Hammersmith from the west get a good view of the remains of

78

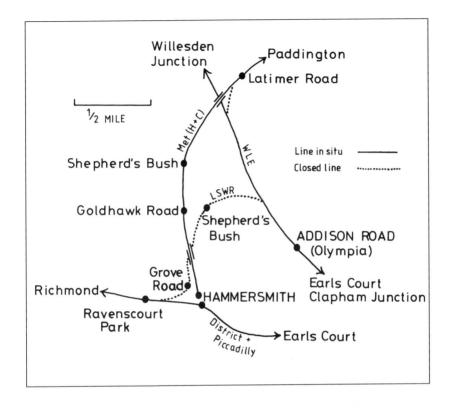

one of West London's shortest-lived railway lines. As the train descends from Ravenscourt Park towards Hammersmith it passes some curious stretches of viaduct apparently leading nowhere. These relics can also be seen from the King's Mall shopping centre car park.

They are almost all that remains of a line that curved round from Addison Road (now Olympia) station almost to Shepherd's Bush Green and then due south to a station in Hammersmith Grove and which then turned sharply west to enable London & South Western, Great Western and Metropolitan Railway services to reach Richmond via Brentford Road (now Gunnersbury). From Hammersmith westwards the new line ran on a long viaduct westwards to Turnham Green, then southwards to Kew Gardens and Richmond.

79

It owed its origins to the complex railway politics of the 1860s when the London & South Western was anxious to keep the lucrative Richmond traffic to itself and to discourage other railway companies from getting a look in.

The LSWR opened the section from Addison Road to Hammersmith (Grove Road) in January 1869. It had one intermediate station at Shepherd's Bush. The building of this line meant that the terminus of the Metropolitan's Hammersmith & City line from Paddington had to be relocated a short distance to the south. The line was part of a new LSWR route from Waterloo to Richmond via Shepherd's Bush and the West London Extension line. The company also provided a rather circuitous service between Richmond and Ludgate Hill via Hammersmith, Addison Road, Clapham Junction and Black-friars – it must have taken most of the morning! It's all rather odd because the LSWR already had a perfectly good route to Richmond via Barnes and Putney, opened in 1846 and still very much with us. From June 1870 a link to the new line from the Hammersmith & City enabled GWR trains to get to Richmond and in 1877 the Metropolitan Railway ran trains from Moorgate to Richmond using this route. A joint GWR-Metropolitan service from Aldgate to Richmond ran from 1894.

Perhaps these routes were a little too devious, seeing that Richmond had the direct LSWR line to Waterloo, the District Railway and the North London services to Broad Street. Shepherd's Bush had better connections via the Central London Underground and the Metropolitan. In any event the competition for passengers following the arrival of electric tram services along King Street in the early years of the 20th century resulted in the link with the Hammersmith & City being closed in 1911.

However, since 1877 the section westwards from Hammer-smith had been used by the District Railway for its own services to Richmond and these continue to this day. This involved the reconstruction of its separate terminus station on Hammersmith Broadway and climbing westwards from there to join the LSWR route east of Shaftesbury Road station (opened 1873, renamed Ravenscourt Park in 1888).

All LSWR services from Richmond to Waterloo followed the direct route via Clapham Junction from 1912. The company was

*An LMS electric unit for Broad Street in the centre bay at Richmond station with a District Line train just visible beyond it. In the foreground are the tracks of Southern Railway's Waterloo to Staines main line. Before the First World War, Richmond was the destination of various long-forgotten services, including one from Waterloo via Kensington (Addison Road), Shepherd's Bush and Hammersmith Grove. (Stations UK)*

reluctant to pull the plug on its Shepherd's Bush line, since it had invested so heavily in promoting and building it, but eventually admitted defeat and all services were withdrawn from 5th June 1916.

For a short stretch of railway that closed around ninety years ago, there is still a surprising amount of evidence to be seen of the Addison Road–Hammersmith section. This is partly because the railway remained intact for many years after closure. It was rumoured that the route might have some strategic importance in time of war so it was safeguarded from development. It was the relatively new Southern Railway (created in the 1923 'Grouping' of railway companies) that eventually decided to dismantle the line in 1926. The first building on the trackbed, a futuristic art-deco block of flats known as 'The Grampians', off Shepherd's Bush Road, was not built until 1937. Grove Road

*Hammersmith (Grove Road), pre-1916. (Hammersmith and Fulham Archives and Local History Centre)*

station and the nearby girder bridge over Hammersmith Grove were demolished in 1954, nearly forty years after closure. The canopies and stairways of Shepherd's Bush station lasted until the late 1950s.

An exploration of the route can begin at the present-day Kensington Olympia station. North of here, where the West London line passes under Addison Gardens, the strip of railway land widens to give room for the Richmond line to branch off. It is noticeable that the road bridge is far longer than would be needed to cross just two tracks. On the north side of Addison Gardens a long block of offices indicates the former trackbed where it curved away to the north-west before beginning its 180 degree turn towards the south.

The next road to cross the line was the significantly-named Richmond Way. There is still a hump in the road and the futuristic-looking Kensington Spa Health and Fitness Club building (K WEST) stands where the trains used to run. In

*Southbound train on the Silverlink Willesden Junction to Clapham Junction line approaching Kensington Olympia (formerly Addison Road). The former LSWR line to Hammersmith branched off to the left beyond the curve in the distance. (Author)*

Rockley Road the flats known as Rockley Court stand on the former railway track somewhat below the level of the road where there used to be another bridge. 'The Grampians', which looks like the setting for one of Agatha Christie's Poirot mysteries, and whose construction finally put paid to any re-use of the line, stands on the east side of Shepherd's Bush Road where a tell-tale rise gives away the site of yet another stretch of track.

Across the road the Sulgrave Gardens flats and lock-up garages are on the site of the former Shepherd's Bush station. Further round there is an attractive row named Railway Cottages in Sulgrave Road. Although they are within sight and sound of trains on the Hammersmith & City, the bus depot is in between, so it is more likely that their name and origin relate to the LSWR branch.

It was near here that the connecting line between the LSWR

branch and the Hammersmith & City ran. The signal box controlling this junction remained in place until the 1970s, close to a number of car-repair premises. From the alleyway from Wells Road it is possible to make out where the old line went underneath the Hammersmith & City route. Beyond, all that remains here now are the abutments for the bridge over Trussley Road.

Of the wide wooden platforms of Grove Road station or of the girder bridge beyond there are no traces, although the brick station building survived in use as a banana warehouse until 1954. The site is now an NCP car park but some local bus routes still start from just outside.

The curve to the west beyond Hammersmith Grove has vanished under the modern shopping centre. Further on though, beyond the multi-storey car park off Glenthorne Road and visible from it, are the impressive remains of the viaduct at the junction with what became the District Line route from Hammersmith. Amazingly it was reconstructed at some cost to

*Railway Cottages, Sulgrave Road, Hammersmith. The LSWR line ran just behind these. (Author)*

84

*Grove Mews sounds an exclusive address, but these houses would have been even closer to the LSWR Hammersmith line than they are to the Metropolitan! (Author)*

allow for one of the extra tracks needed for the Piccadilly Line extension here in the 1930s. This despite the fact that no trains had used the viaduct since 1916! On westwards through Ravenscourt Park, Stamford Brook and Turnham Green run the District and Piccadilly tracks, utilising the low viaduct built by the LSWR for its line to Richmond. How many harassed commuters travelling this line daily realise that it is part of a route with such a complicated history!

# Latimer Road to Shepherd's Bush

The Hammersmith & City had another link in this area. Just south of Latimer Road station a line branched off to link up with the West London line at Shepherd's Bush. A small part of its

85

viaduct is visible from trains heading towards Hammersmith but the rest of it was demolished for the construction of the motorway.

The original Shepherd's Bush station on the Hammersmith & City (opened with the line in 1864) was on the viaduct between the present Goldhawk Road and Shepherd's Bush stations. The booking hall was in one of the arches of the viaduct. When the line was electrified in 1906 it was decided to replace this station with two more conveniently placed ones but Goldhawk Road and the new Shepherd's Bush stations did not open until April 1914. The platforms, trackside buildings and stairways were soon demolished but the former booking hall in the arch of the viaduct remains and now serves as the office for the market that still exists in the shadow of the railway viaduct.

*The still-impressive remains of the LSWR viaduct linking its line from Addison Road via Shepherd's Bush to the District and Piccadilly Line west of Hammersmith. View from King's Mall car park. (Nicholas Battle)*

# 7

# On The Met In Middlesex

## *Metroland's ghost stations*

The word 'Metroland' will always be associated with the Metropolitan Railway in Middlesex and the writings of John Betjeman. The Metropolitan tracks through Finchley Road, Harrow-on-the-Hill and Pinner to Uxbridge and Amersham are not, of course, 'Lost Lines' but along the route north-westwards from Baker Street there are a number of ghost stations, traces of which remain if you know where to look.

Cricket fans once had the benefit of a Metropolitan Railway station closer to Lord's than the present St John's Wood on the Bakerloo. This was opened by the 'Metropolitan & St John's Wood Railway Company' in April 1868 and soon became very busy, especially during the cricket season. It was named 'St John's Wood Road' and was close to the junction with Park Road. It was rebuilt in 1925 when the word 'Road' was deleted from the station name. It was renamed 'Lord's' in June 1939 at the suggestion of the MCC but, with the onset of war, it closed a few months later and never reopened.

The main reason was in fact not the war but the opening of the Bakerloo Line extension with its deep-level St John's Wood tube station. It had been intended that the Met station might reopen just on match days but it was badly damaged by bombs in November 1940, which put paid to that idea. The impressive street level station building of 1925 survived on the south side of St John's Wood Road until the late 1960s.

A little further along the line was Marlborough Road station at the corner of Finchley Road and Queen's Grove. Never much used, it was also a victim of the opening of St John's Wood station on the Bakerloo on 20th November 1939 and closed on

*Preston Road station on the route out to 'Metroland', 1972. This view shows the typical development of shops with flats above that grew up around some stations during the inter-war years. (Stations UK)*

the same day. The glass overall roof, supported on curved iron girders identical to those at Lord's and Swiss Cottage Metropolitan stations, survived more or less intact until 1966 and the street level building, used as a restaurant since the 1970s, can still be seen. The outline of the former roof can be traced on the back wall of the station building.

The old platforms can be seen from passing trains and in 1973 appeared in Sir John Betjeman's classic television odyssey *Metroland* with the Poet Laureate standing there mournfully. 'This is all that is left of Marlborough Road station,' he intoned. 'Up there the iron brackets supported the glass and iron roof. And you see that white house up there? That was where Thomas Hood died. Thomas Hood the poet. He wrote "I remember, I remember, the house where I was born", and the railway cut

88

through his garden.' He went on, 'I remember Marlborough Road station because it was the nearest station to the house where lived my future parents-in-law.' The impoverished young poet's relationship with the formidable Major-General Chetwode of the Indian Army was not good and we could imagine his feelings of anxiety as he alighted at Marlborough Road on his way to ask for their beloved daughter Penelope's hand in marriage.

Swiss Cottage was the country terminus of the Metropolitan Railway between April 1868 and June 1879 when the extension to West Hampstead was opened. It stood at the corner of Finchley Road and Belsize Road. Once again, the Bakerloo extension to Finchley Road in 1939 killed off the Met station. There had been plans for a Met-Bakerloo interchange at Swiss Cottage, but nothing came of them. Very little now survives of the old Metropolitan station, although, once again, remains of the old platforms can be seen from passing trains.

Preston Road is another one of those stations that have been relocated. A simple halt was opened in May 1908 as 'Preston Road for Uxendon'. Like Runemede (later Yeoveney) halt on the GWR Staines branch, it was originally built largely to serve firing ranges, in this case those of the Uxendon Shooting School Club.

Again like Runemede it was in a remote rural area and trains only called by request. Engine drivers sometimes failed to notice waiting passengers and the train would go through without stopping. It was decided that intending passengers would be accompanied onto the wooden platforms by the booking clerk. The poor man would have to leave his cosy little office and, red flag in hand, come down the steps to the bleak, bare platform to stop the train. It does not seem to have been much of an economy.

As Metroland began to be built up in the 1920s this provision became increasingly inadequate. During 1930 the Metropolitan Line between Wembley Park and Harrow-on-the Hill was widened from two tracks to four. Preston Road station was rebuilt on the opposite side of the road bridge and the old halt was dismantled. It was such a basic structure that no traces of it remain.

Beyond Amersham and Aylesbury the Metropolitan reached

out into rural Buckinghamshire to Quainton Road (now the site of a preserved railway operation), Verney Junction and the single-track Brill Branch – surely the most primitive outpost of London Transport in the 1930s, but sadly well beyond the Middlesex border and so outside the scope of this book.

# 8
# Exhibition Traffic

### *'We're going to Wember-lee!'*
### *Wood Lane*

*Wembley Exhibition station. (Peter Rousselange, Wembley History Society)*

## 'We're going to Wember-lee!'

Football fans and other sports enthusiasts with a sense of history have fond memories of Wembley Stadium. Its subsequent years of dereliction and the long-running shambles of its redevelopment does no-one involved any credit.

The stadium was one of the buildings put up in the 1920s for the British Empire Exhibition of 1924-5 – the Millennium Dome of its day. In 1924 the London & North Eastern Railway opened a special loop line and station to serve the complex. Like the

Heathrow Loop at the end of the Piccadilly Line today, the loop was traversed in one direction, enabling trains to turn round without stopping to reverse.

The Wembley Exhibition Loop was about a mile long and diverged from the line out of Marylebone just west of Neasden. It had the latest in colour-light signalling. Wembley Exhibition station was fittingly in the art-deco style that was, in a popular phrase of the time, 'the bee's knees'! It had a single concrete platform and could accommodate a train of up to eight coaches. The massive futuristic Palace of Engineering was linked to the loop line by a series of sidings. Among the wonders on display were the Flying Scotsman locomotive of the LNER, claimed to be the most powerful passenger engine in Britain. The Great Western Railway disputed this and had their Caerphilly Castle on an adjacent stand. One wonders whether the custodians of these competing exhibits ever came to blows!

After the exhibition closed many of the buildings were demolished but, like the Festival Hall after 1951, Wembley Stadium was intended to be a permanent reminder of a great

*Wembley Park station, c1925. Notice the old-style station sign, destined to be replaced in the 1930s when the innovative Frank Pick introduced the familiar London Transport roundel. (Stations UK)*

*Soon after nationalisation, British Railways 2-6-0 locomotive no 31905 is photographed at Wembley Hill with a train bringing supporters of Bromley football club to the FA Amateur Cup Final on 23rd April 1949. (John H. Meredith)*

occasion. Cup Finals and other big events were staged there and in 1948 the loop saw big crowds over an extended period when the first post-war Olympic Games were held at the stadium. The station was by now named after the stadium rather than the exhibition.

A big event, such as the 1948 Cup Final between Manchester United and Blackpool, pulled in 100,000 spectators, most of whom came by public transport. Trains would leave Marylebone every eight minutes for the short journey to Wembley and on these days eight trains plus a spare locomotive would be needed.

Travel patterns changed in the 1960s and, with more spectators coming to Wembley by car, the need for a special line – not earning revenue for most days of the year when there was no service – decreased. There were never any regular passenger trains otherwise and, of course, the area was well served by stations on other lines. The last train ran on the loop in

May 1968 although the line did not officially close until September 1969.

Wembley Stadium station was demolished in 1974 and the area was comprehensively redeveloped so that there are few traces left of what was one of the shortest, most unusual and shortest-lived of the lost railways of Middlesex. However, the curving course of the line is clearly visible on air photographs and can, with some difficulty, still be traced on foot. It curved away from the line between Neasden and Wembley Park, running parallel with Fourth Way in the Business Park. It then ran to the west of Second Way, the curve of the road following the alignment of the railway and a gap in the buildings making it clear where the trains once ran. There is still a concrete bridge parapet in South Way where it crossed the branch just before its junction with the line from Wembley Hill (later confusingly renamed Wembley Stadium) to Marylebone. Not much to show for what was once something of a showpiece!

# Wood Lane

Back in 1908 the Franco-British Exhibition was held at a site in West London close to the Central London Railway's depot at Wood Lane. To take advantage of the extra passenger traffic expected the railway company decided to extend its line from its terminus at Shepherd's Bush to a special exhibition station near the depot. A sharply-curved loop was constructed and the new station was opened on 14th May 1908 to coincide with the start of the exhibition.

An ornate bridge carried a pedestrian walkway from the station over Wood Lane to the exhibition grounds. A promotional leaflet was produced advertising the CLR as 'The Direct Line to the Franco-British Exhibition'. The cover featured Britannia and the Spirit of France carrying their national flags and being conveyed by propeller-driven airship above the London skyline. The reality inside was somewhat more prosaic – a map of the underground route from Bank (including the now-forgotten Post Office and British Museum stations) and

94

times of the first and last trains (5 am until half-past midnight on weekdays; 8 am to 11.30 pm on Sundays).

The station remained in use after the exhibition closed on 31st October and in 1915, two years after the CLR became part of the Underground Group, it was reconstructed. It was rebuilt again in 1920 when the Central Line extension to Ealing Broadway was opened. Two underground platforms were added to the two on the surface. A curiosity of the surface station was the moveable section added in 1928 to the east end of the platform for trains from the City. This was needed when longer trains were introduced on the line. When an incoming train needed to be run into the depot this section could be swung clear of the points to enable this to be done.

Access to the station was still dependent on the old single-track loop from Shepherd's Bush. This was a very inconvenient bottle-neck and in November 1947 White City station was opened to replace Wood Lane. However, the eastbound platform of the old station can still be seen from passing trains. The former station entrance from the street, dating from the 1915 rebuilding, survives but there are plans to preserve this in the London Transport Museum Depot at Acton.

The Central London Railway was not the only one to have an eye on the Franco-British Exhibition traffic. The Metropolitan also opened a station on the Hammersmith & City branch. Known as Wood Lane (Exhibition) station, it was advertised as 'The only station in the grounds'. The Metropolitan stole a march on the CLR by opening their station a fortnight earlier.

Despite this the station had a rather chequered history. It was closed in November 1914 and not reopened until 5th November 1920 when, as 'Wood Lane (White City)', it was opened for just the day for a motor show. Trains thereafter stopped on occasional days for special events, mainly greyhound racing at the White City Stadium. In November 1940 the railway viaduct and part of the eastbound platform were damaged in an air-raid.

The station was renamed White City in 1947 but on 25th October 1959 there was a bad fire and the station never reopened. It was demolished in 1961. However, early in 2002 London Transport announced plans for a new Wood Lane station to be built on the Hammersmith & City line.

# 9

# The Hotelier's Line

## Stanmore via Belmont

*Stanmore branch train waiting to leave the terminus on the return trip to Harrow & Wealdstone, May 1934. (Ken Nunn Collection, the Locomotive Club of Great Britain/Harrow Local History Collection)*

The London & North Western Railway's two mile branch from Harrow & Wealdstone to Stanmore owes its existence to a successful entrepreneur used to getting his own way. In 1882 London hotelier Frederick Gordon, developer of land alongside Northumberland Avenue, bought the impressive mansion of Bentley Priory at Great Stanmore with a view to developing the

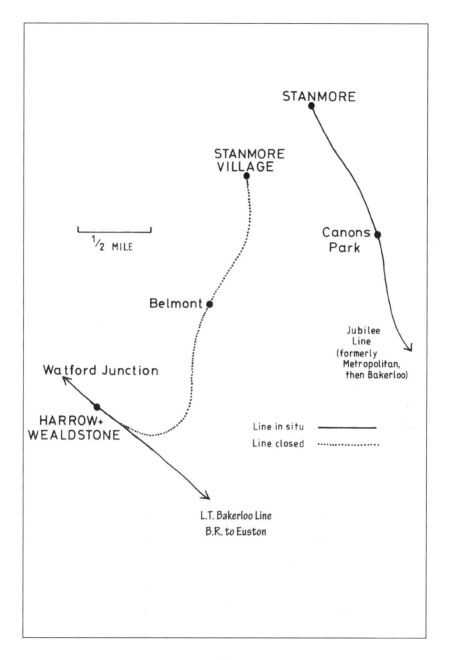

STANMORE

STANMORE
VILLAGE

¹/₂ MILE

Canons
Park

Belmont

Jubilee
Line
(formerly
Metropolitan,
then Bakerloo)

Watford Junction

HARROW+
WEALDSTONE

Line in situ    ————
Line closed     ·····················

L.T. Bakerloo Line
B.R. to Euston

estate into what would nowadays be described as a Hotel and Country Club. The estate was well-wooded and attractive – for Gordon's purposes it lacked only one thing: easy access by rail.

Gordon decided to promote a branch from the main line station at Harrow & Wealdstone. Raising the capital was quite a task, even for a man in his privileged position. There were a number of disappointments but in December 1890, after an agreement with the LNWR to maintain and operate the line, the Stanmore branch opened.

It was a genteel little operation. Gordon was well aware of the importance of keeping on the right side of his neighbours in this exclusive residential district. Trains started in mid-morning and finished in the early evening, making the service unsuitable for any of the lower classes who might be tempted to use it to get to their menial jobs. There were no Sunday trains. Stanmore station was expensively designed and detailed to fit in with the architectural pretensions of the area. Constructed of homely red-brick and tile, its tower and spire gave it the look of a country church rather than a mundane railway station. It stood at the junction of Gordon Road (presumably named after the line's promoter) and Old Church Lane.

*The Gothic splendour of Stanmore Village terminus. (Harrow Local History Collection)*

98

Unfortunately for Mr Gordon the line was unable to prevent his ambitious hotel scheme at Bentley Priory from being a failure. He lived in it with his large family for a few years and after his death it became a school for young ladies. Neither was there any significant housing development in the area before the 1920s. The new bus services locally took what little traffic there was and funnelled it to the Northern Line terminus at nearby Edgware, which provided a cheaper and more frequent service to London. When the main line station at Harrow & Wealdstone was rebuilt by the LNWR in 1912, the position of the Stanmore tracks and the junction facing away from London made it uneconomic to electrify the branch and key it into the improved suburban service into Euston. The future of the branch was far from rosy.

However, it was when the area began to go relatively downmarket in the late twenties and early thirties that the line's prospects improved. A limited number of well-heeled professionals were never going to provide enough revenue but in the twenties areas to the east of the line, in the districts around

*Stanmore Village terminus, during the inter-war years, seems deserted. The single-coach trains look more than adequate for the number of passengers travelling along the branch to Harrow & Wealdstone via Belmont. (Stations UK)*

*This picture first appeared in the 'Harrow Observer', 16th September 1932, with the caption, 'The new Belmont Halt, which has been opened midst rural surroundings this week'. The surrounding area is now largely built-up but the wooded slopes in the background are part of Stanmore golf course (Harrow Local History Collection)*

Kenton and Belmont, began to be sold off for the building of modest terraces and semis. The developers were keen to see the improved transport links which would help their sales and persuaded the LNWR to open a little halt in September 1932 at the point where Kenton Lane crossed the branch. This rapidly became the main generator of passenger traffic and in 1937 the station was reconstructed and provided with a heated waiting room. The frequency of trains improved steadily during the 1930s to meet the extra demand.

Stanmore LNWR station, despite its architectural quality, missed out on all this. The Metropolitan Line had built a new Stanmore station in a more accessible position a short distance away, the terminus of a branch from Wembley Park that was to become successively part of the Bakerloo and then the Jubilee lines. It was no surprise when services between Belmont and Stanmore were withdrawn on 11th September 1952, only two years after British Railways had taken the trouble to rename the terminus Stanmore Village and gone to the expense of providing new station signs!

Just a month later there occurred at Harrow & Wealdstone station one of Britain's worst railway disasters. On a foggy morning a late-running Perth to Euston sleeping car express ploughed into the back of the 7.31 am Tring to Euston stopping train which had just stopped to pick up more passengers from the crowded platform. The last three coaches of the stopping train were compressed into the length of just one. The Harrow signalman witnessed this carnage and did his best to stop the 8 am Euston to Liverpool express from running into the wreckage from the opposite direction. He was too late. The Liverpool train, fifteen coaches hauled by two steam locomotives, was travelling at 60 miles an hour as it reached the station just after the first impact and it was unable to stop; 112 people were killed at the scene and ten died later from their injuries. A compacted mass of wreckage 45 yards long, 18 yards wide and 30 feet high was wedged between the station platforms.

Confidence in the safety of rail travel was shaken and the name 'Harrow & Wealdstone' appeared in sombre black headlines in newspapers, just as Lewisham, Clapham and Ladbroke Grove were later to do. The quiet stub-end branch, now just running to Belmont, seemed very remote from the devastation at the junction but for some folk their last journey must have started uneventfully on Belmont's island platform, to which they had fully expected to return that night. Others, perhaps, who had changed their travel arrangements and begun to travel from Stanmore by tube instead must have felt that fate was on their side.

Afterwards, the little diesel train continued to shuttle between Belmont and Harrow for another twelve years until 3rd October 1964 when the line was closed. By then the train fares were considerably higher than on the competing bus routes – seen by many as a cynical ploy by BR management to make the line uneconomical enough to justify closure. Outside the rush hours

*Aerial view of Harrow & Wealdstone station in the aftermath of the 1952 crash.*
*site. The north is to the left; London (Euston) is to the right. (Planet News Ltd/*

*Stanmore Village branch trains used the platform at top right of the station*
*Harrow Local History Collection)*

*Special 'last train' at Belmont station, 1964. The notice to the right lists the very limited opening hours of the station by that time. (Harrow Local History Collection)*

there were virtually no passengers. An enterprising 15 year old schoolboy who collected 1,080 signatures on a petition against closure had to admit to the closure enquiry that only 450 were regular users of the line.

There's not much left to see. At Harrow & Wealdstone station, which has recently been attractively restored, the Stanmore branch platform remains in place on the eastern side but there has been no track alongside it probably since the 1960s. Beyond the road bridge the trackbed has disappeared under commercial development.

The streets around Harrow & Wealdstone station are devoid of charm – a world away from genteel Harrow-on-the-Hill. A drab walk along Masons Avenue and past the Leisure Centre brings you to Christchurch Avenue where the site of the railway overbridge can be identified. The trackbed continues northwards behind the houses of Kenmore Avenue. There is a muddy and overgrown footpath (but probably not a right-of-way) along the top of the embankment but it would take a very determined enthusiast to force his way through. Kenmore Avenue provides an easier, though unexciting, alternative to reach the site of Belmont station.

Belmont Circle is the centre of a residential area that developed here between the wars and gave the moribund branch a new lease of life. Nowadays, judging by the range of newspapers on sale in the shop and the traditional music on offer in the pubs, one of which is called the Lough, there must be a sizeable Irish community living in the district.

The surroundings of the old station site are a disgrace. It is approached through a scruffy car park on former railway land. A large sign by the Kenton Lane bridge reads 'No Tipping' but as so often this merely serves to mark the centre of a trail of rubbish and refuse that stretches along the track back towards Harrow. The trackbed is traceable but this stretch looks no more promising for walkers than it did from Christchurch Avenue.

*Harrow & Wealdstone station looking north. The Stanmore branch trains departed from the fenced-off platform to the right. (Author)*

Things are a little better in the opposite direction. At the end of the car park another sign informs the visitor that what lies ahead is part of the Belmont Nature Walk run by the London Wildlife Trust. The path here runs for about a quarter of a mile in a slight cutting with trees and undergrowth on both sides as far as Wemborough Road. Beyond, the branch continued along the eastern boundary of Stanmore golf course for about half a mile to the terminus.

There is nothing to see there now. The station area has been totally redeveloped although the track can perhaps be discerned as a line of trees at the end of a cul-de-sac called September Way. The picturesque station was demolished but some fragments of the ornamental stonework were incorporated in a new house, somewhat incongruously named 'The Old Station', which was built on the site. From here it is about ten minutes' walk to the Stanmore (London Transport) station which superseded it.

# 10
# Lost Stations On The Piccadilly Line

*Indecision at Hounslow*
*Osterley, Northfields, Park Royal and north-east*
*to Cockfosters*

*Hounslow Town terminus (District Railway). Hounslow bus station now stands on this site at the eastern end of the High Street. (Hounslow Library Service, Local Studies Collection)*

## Indecision at Hounslow

Hounslow bus station is one of the most important interchanges in the public transport system of West London. Very few of the

107

thousands who use it each day, however, will be aware that it stands on the site of the former terminus of the erstwhile Hounslow & Metropolitan Railway, opened in 1883.

From the start this line was operated as part of the Metropolitan District Railway (now the Piccadilly Line) from the City and West End via Earl's Court and the intention was to extend it southwards to join up with the London & South Western Railway's Kingston Loop between Twickenham and Strawberry Hill. The MDR had plans to use this extension to tap the lucrative market provided by the well-heeled residents of the Twickenham and Kingston areas. There were grandiose plans for a circular service to and from Earl's Court via Hounslow, Kingston, Wimbledon and Fulham.

The LSWR resisted this invasion of its territory and the MDR's plans did not get parliamentary approval. The terminus at Hounslow remained as a relic of this plan. Reached by a 20-arch brick viaduct, the station, at the eastern end of Hounslow High Street, was at a higher level than the road and obviously built with the intention of extending the tracks southwards towards

*Long before the extension to Heathrow was dreamed of, a westbound Piccadilly Line train leaves Hounslow East station bound for the terminus at Hounslow West via Hounslow Central. (Stations UK)*

Twickenham. There were two side platforms and a station house at street level. Alan A. Jackson in *London's Local Railways* writes of 'the rails pointing menacingly towards the first-class riverside territory of the LSWR'. Work was started on a bridge over the High Street, abutments were built – but that was all.

In 1884 the line was extended, not south but westwards, from Lampton Junction to Hounslow Barracks (later Hounslow West). After less than a year then, Hounslow Town found itself at the dead-end of an awkward little appendix that led nowhere and would not have been built at all but for the ill-fated ambition of the Metropolitan District Railway. It was closed at the end of March 1886 after less than three years' use. To serve this part of the town the MDR opened a Heston-Hounslow station on the single-line extension to Hounslow Barracks. This was in Lampton Road, only half a mile to the west, but a good deal less convenient for the town centre.

In 1901 a contributor to the *Railway Magazine* described visiting the derelict remains of Hounslow Town station and finding washing hanging from the supports of the canopies, chickens roaming the platforms and council dustcarts and steamrollers stored in the station yard and the arches of the viaduct.

The whole of the Hounslow line was somewhat run-down at this time. The railway company had not promoted the area for residential development in the way that the Metropolitan Railway was later to do for 'Metroland'. The train service was poor – only one train an hour – and the stations badly maintained.

However, the introduction of electric tram services to Brentford and Hounslow provoked the railway into action. Hounslow Town station was reopened on 1st March 1903 with a service of two trains per hour, more at peak times. Other improvements along the line stimulated building development around Hounslow, Ealing and Northfields and revenue increased.

For the introduction of electric trains in June 1905 a new spur was constructed enabling trains to run from Hounslow Town to Heston-Hounslow without having to reverse at Lampton Junction. However, it was still a nuisance having to run into

109

Hounslow Town and out again and the line to the original terminus was closed on the evening of 1st May 1909. From the next morning its place was taken by a new station, just 300 yards north but on the through line to the Barracks where it crossed Kingsley Road. This bore the name Hounslow Town like its predecessor but was renamed Hounslow East in 1925.

The old station site was redeveloped as a bus garage for the London General Omnibus Company and opened in 1912. The present bus station was built in 1954 – still that inconvenient 300 yards from Hounslow East tube station when it might have been possible to create a useful transport interchange on a bigger site. A plaque put up by the local historical society is all there is to inform passengers that there was once a station here but the curve of a footpath leading from the back of the bus depot to the railway bridge in Spring Grove Road runs next to an overgrown fragment of the old alignment.

# Osterley, Northfields, Park Royal and north-east to Cockfosters

Travelling into London from Hounslow's various stations on the Piccadilly Line today the passenger soon arrives at Osterley, a modern-style station on the Great West Road, opened in March 1934. This replaced the original station, sometimes known more fully as 'Osterley & Spring Grove', which was a short distance further east with an entrance from the Thornbury Road overbridge. Thornbury Road gives access to Osterley Park and was the logical place to put the station back in 1883, long before the rows of thirties' semis covered the fields and before the Great West Road was even a line on the planners' map. Osterley & Spring Grove station had lengthy canopies protecting passengers on its slightly curving platforms. These canopies were not demolished (along with the stairways which gave access to the platforms) until 1957. The platforms remain and can be easily seen from the train. Up on Thornbury Road the original station house and booking office still survive, latterly used as a second-hand bookshop. I wonder how many browsers among the books

110

*The original station house at Osterley (now a bookshop). The tracks pass under the bridge in the background. (Author)*

realise that they are standing where Victorian and Edwardian commuters purchased their season tickets.

Just along the line Northfields station has also been relocated. The original station was to the west of the road bridge and was opened as 'Northfield (Ealing) Halt' in 1908. The lack of promotion of services on the Hounslow line had held back suburban development until that time and even then only a very basic halt was provided by the parsimonious Metropolitan District Railway. There were just the two platforms and a street-level ticket hut, constructed out of corrugated iron, perched rather precariously on the side of the road bridge.

It was probably a false economy as increasing traffic meant that the halt had to be rebuilt more substantially by 1911 when the station was renamed 'Northfields & Little Ealing'. Even this had a comparatively short life. The laying of additional tracks from Acton Town for the Piccadilly service which paralleled the District Line service from 1932, and also the building of the new train depot between Northfields and Boston Manor, meant that it was replaced by a new four-platform station, opened on 19th May of that year, to the east of the bridge. Northfields station is now so close to South Ealing that you can see the platforms of one from the other and the train has barely got up speed before it has to slow down and stop once again.

One of the most romantically-named stations, which totally failed to live up to the images its name conjured up, was 'Park Royal & Twyford Abbey' on the branch of the Piccadilly Line to South Harrow and Uxbridge. Like the first Northfields it was built originally by the Metropolitan District Railway and boasted one of its mean little corrugated iron ticket offices, two bare wooden platforms and little else.

The station was on the south side of Twyford Abbey Road and

*Northfields station, rebuilt in 1932, is a modernist design by architect Charles Holden. The Metropolitan District Railway had opened a halt known as Northfield (Ealing) on 16 April 1908. With increased development in the area, this soon proved inadequate and was rebuilt as Northfields & Little Ealing station in 1911. When the Piccadilly Line service to Hounslow was extended, extra tracks and a depot were needed, necessitating the re-siting of Northfields station to the opposite side of Northfield Avenue bridge. (Stations UK)*

was opened on 22nd June 1903 to serve the large Royal Agricultural Showground. Unfortunately for the railway company – and the show's organisers – it rained so hard that the earthworks of the new line shifted and on the opening day of the show only a limited shuttle service from Mill Hill Park (now Acton Town) was possible. Things were better for the rest of the week of the show but attendance was the lowest for 28 years. Despite the new electric trains and also a Great Western steam service, the Royal Agricultural Society gave up using Park Royal in 1905. For a while the area continued to be used as sports grounds but later became the site of the Park Royal Industrial Estate. The halt's story is similar to those of Osterley and Northfields.

Writing in 1908, the Rev W.J. Scott, one-time Anglo-Catholic Vicar of St Saviour's church, Upper Sunbury and a director of the Great Western Railway, wrote that 'since the closing of the Agricultural Showground, Park Royal station has sunk to the level of a halt on ordinary days. On Saturdays throughout the winter, however, great crowds alight on its platforms for the football field. The football traffic is too great to be dealt with by mere rail motors so special trains, some off foreign companies' lines, are run for the association matches.' In the same article, incidentally, Father Scott describes nearby Northolt as 'the most rustic village in "Wild West" Middlesex'!

When the route was taken over by the Piccadilly Line in 1932 it was decided to build a new Park Royal station further along the line, alongside Western Avenue. There is now nothing left of the little halt in Twyford Abbey Road.

The Piccadilly Line crosses the old county of Middlesex from west to north. The stations on the extension through North Middlesex to Cockfosters were better sited and have all survived but the route across London passes through three other closed stations of which some traces can be seen: Brompton Road (between Knightsbridge and South Kensington), Down Street (between Dover Street – now Green Park – and Hyde Park Corner) and York Road (between King's Cross and Caledonian Road). All three of these underground stations suffered from poor passenger numbers due to the proximity of other, more conveniently-located, stations. All were missed out by some

113

trains and all were closed in the early 1930s. The familiar surface buildings with their blood-red tiles and round-headed arches still survive and the locations of their underground platforms stations can be recognised by the tube passenger by the change in the pitch of the sound of the train rumbling through the tunnels.

# 11
# Ally Pally Palaver

*The Great Northern route from Finsbury Park*
*An electric pioneer*
*To the Palace Gates by GER*

*Alexandra Palace Station. This photo must have been taken in 1891-2 during the short period when the station was known as Alexandra Park. (Hornsey Historical Society)*

# The Great Northern route from Finsbury Park

## North London's Great White Elephant

Alexandra Palace, North London's rival to the Crystal Palace, could perhaps be described as a Great White Elephant rather than a Great White Hope. Named after the new Princess of Wales, wife of the future King Edward VII, and opened with great fanfare on 24th May 1873, the building was badly damaged by fire on 9th June.

According to *The Illustrated London News* 'the cause of the fire was the carelessness of workmen employed to repair the leadwork in the roof of the great dome. A morsel of red hot charcoal dropped from a brazier set fire to the timber and paper mache while the men were gone to dinner. In a few minutes, almost before the alarm could be given, the flames spread in every direction till the whole vast building was consumed.'

This was a bit of an exaggeration but panic followed as visitors escaped from the building and staff attempted to rescue the works of art on display. The pictures were hastily torn from the walls and carried along lines of men out into the safety of the park. Fighting the flames was not aided by the discovery that high up on the hill there was not sufficient pressure of water from the hydrants for the hoses to be operated effectively.

The palace was badly damaged and did not reopen until May 1875. Even then it was unable to pay its way and further closures followed, from August 1882 until March 1885 and between September 1885 and May 1889.

All this was bad news for the Great Northern and Great Eastern Railway Companies who both invested heavily in building lines to take the happy punters up to the 'Ally Pally'. So concerned was the Great Northern to protect its investment that, on hearing news of the outbreak of the fire, it had immediately dispatched two of its own fire appliances by rail from King's Cross. The fact that these arrived at the scene before the local fire brigade does not say much for the service offered by the fire brigades of Wood Green and Muswell Hill!

116

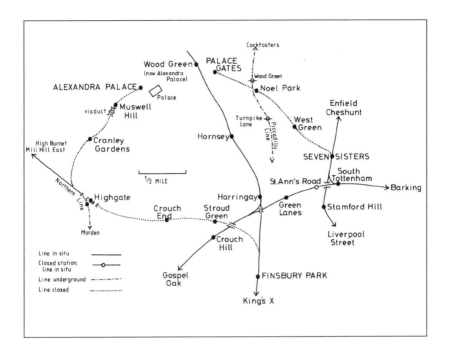

For a short while after the fire a reduced service was run by the GNR for the benefit of sightseers who wanted to gawp at the blackened ruins. The novelty soon wore off.

It was only after the turn of the century, when suburban development began to fill the fields around Wood Green, Muswell Hill and Crouch End, that these lines began to show anything like a profit but soon afterwards competition from more frequent and reliable bus services began to eat into these profits and both lines are now just memories in the minds of older residents.

More of the Great Eastern line later. The Great Northern's had a chequered history, almost found prosperity as an extension of the London Underground system and much of the route today is a highly-valued linear park and footpath through a densely built up part of North London.

The GNR had opened a line from Seven Sisters Road (later renamed Finsbury Park) to Crouch End and Highgate in 1867

117

*Crouch End station, c1910. (Dick Whetstone, Hornsey Historical Society)*

and this was later extended to Edgware (of which more in Chapter 12) and to Barnet. As plans for the Alexandra Palace at long last seemed likely to bear fruit, work began on a branch from Highgate, through Muswell Hill, to a station in the shadow of the Palace itself. The line was served not only by GNR trains from King's Cross but also by North London Railway services from Broad Street via Canonbury.

Highgate station had originally been intended as an intermediate terminus on the main line to Edgware. It was situated in a cutting with tunnels at either end. The two platforms were built sufficiently far apart for a siding to run between the two lines. Increasing traffic led to rebuilding around 1880 when the side platforms were replaced by a central island platform. Access to the station was from a booking office on the footbridge which led to street entrances on both sides of the tracks.

The early days of the line were somewhat fraught. The Palace's financial problems were reflected in various temporary suspensions of the rail service and when the crowds did come the railway was often unable to cope with them. On Whit Monday

*Muswell Hill station (GNR) opened in 1873. (Hornsey Historical Society)*

1875 there were 94,000 visitors to Alexandra Palace, most of them coming by rail. It took an hour or more to get there from King's Cross and a derailment in the evening at Copenhagen Tunnel, on the approach to the London terminus, caused a jam back up the branch. Some unfortunates had to spend the night on the trains, which cannot have endeared the new line to them.

The Great Northern had hoped to encourage more of the local residents to use the line. When it reopened in March 1891, after one of its all-too-frequent periods of disuse, the name of the terminus was changed to Alexandra Park, to emphasise the locality rather than the Palace. This was not a great success, however, and the line closed again in April 1892. When it reopened once more in 1898 the station had reverted to its original name of Alexandra Palace.

# Some regular passengers at last!

From 1900 suburban development in the district signalled a revival in the line's fortunes. There was already an intermediate station at Muswell Hill but in August 1902 Cranley Gardens was opened between there and Highgate. Not only did this speculative building produce lots more passengers, it also increased the freight revenues as the building materials were mostly brought in by rail. This was the line's 'Golden Age'. During the First World War the use of the Palace as a holding base for army reservists, then as a centre for Belgian refugees and finally as an internment camp for enemy aliens generated much-needed extra revenue at a time when the GNR had already felt the chill winds of efficient tram and bus competition.

By 1914 the London General Omnibus Company's route 111, linking Muswell Hill and Crouch End with Finsbury Park, was already siphoning off desperately-needed railway passengers. To deal with this the GNR took the risky step of taking its competitors to court, claiming that their buses were causing an excessive strain on the bridges over the railway. All the bus company did was to use smaller buses running more frequently!

After the war the Palace and adjacent park reopened to the public. A boy scout rally in October 1922 saw 60,000 passengers arrive by train. However, all was not well with the GNR branch. In 1924 the *Hornsey Journal* reported that Alexandra Park station was 'dirty, dark and dismal. The trains are so infrequent that this means of access scarcely counts on the few days when crowds are expected. Everyone avoids the station who can possibly do so, for the railway does not even offer the attraction of cheapness.'

Hardly a glowing testimonial!

In the early 1930s, despite the obvious potential, there was no Sunday service on the branch, by now part of the London & North Eastern Railway. On one bank holiday a survey found that out of 30,000 day trippers only about 150 had come to Alexandra Palace by train.

# Hopes of better things

In 1935, however, came hope of better things. It was proposed that the lines from Finsbury Park to High Barnet, Edgware and Alexandra Palace be electrified for tube trains running from Moorgate via Drayton Park with at least six trains per hour going to Alexandra Palace. Highgate would become a two-level station with the tube platforms below the GNR station, which was to be rebuilt in modern style. The tube trains would come to the surface north of the station to link up with the existing rails.

The BBC's use of Alexandra Palace for its fledgling television service in the London area must also have raised hopes for the future and brought more publicity to the line. On one occasion, which must have delighted local railway enthusiasts, two impressive main-line express locomotives, a Gresley Pacific and an Ivatt Atlantic, steamed up to the branch terminus for a special television programme. What a gem that would be if it could be discovered lurking in the TV archives.

Work on the so-called 'Northern Heights' electrification scheme was well advanced at the outbreak of war in September 1939. There had been a Press Preview held on 28th July where Lord Ashfield, Chairman of the London Passenger Transport Board, and Sir Ronald Matthews, Chairman of the LNER, had acted as hosts. Sir Ronald had driven a special train from Archway station to East Finchley and the party of VIPs inspected the still incomplete Highgate station. Lunch was taken at the White Lion, which had been resited to enable the railway bridge there to be widened.

The new extensions had been included in the famous pocket Underground maps from 1938. The 1939 map, headed 'New in London', announced that tube trains were expected to be running on the Alexandra Palace branch by the autumn of 1940.

However, the war brought about a curtailment of this ambitious electrification programme. The new underground platforms at Highgate had not been ready for service when the Northern Line extension to East Finchley had been opened on 3rd July 1939 and the trains had passed through the station without stopping. When the war began in earnest these platforms were pressed into service as air-raid shelters. Trains began to stop for the convenience of shelterers after September 1940 and a full public service began in January 1941.

The line to Barnet received its new service in April 1940 but the GNR Edgware branch was only electrified as far as Mill Hill East and the Alexandra Palace line never saw its tube trains. A lot of the preparatory work had been completed and had the start of the war been delayed by as little as twelve months it is likely that

LT Northern Line trains might have been working over the Palace branch for the last sixty years!

# Post-war decline and closure

As it was, progressive cuts and economies left the Alexandra Palace line in a sorry state after the war. Despite the availability of through bookings from all London Transport stations (introduced in anticipation of the use of tube trains on the branch), the limited nature of the service discouraged passengers. The introduction of a fare scheme based on mileage travelled worked against the line because of its circuitous route. Fares to Alexandra Palace from King's Cross were about half as much again as on the quicker service to the main line Wood Green station nearby. Services were infrequent, off-peak trains were withdrawn and it was no surprise when London Transport formally abandoned their electrification plans for the branch in 1953. Some of the conductor rails had been removed in 1952 for

*The quiet suburbs around Cranley Gardens station are disturbed by the Alexandra Palace branch train. The station was west of Muswell Hill Road and a parade of shops, now looking slightly out of place, is the only sign of its location. (Stations UK)*

122

*The leafy setting of Muswell Hill station. Placed a minute's walk from the Broadway, Muswell Hill was the busiest station on the branch, although it would not appear so from this picture taken a few years before closure. (Stations UK)*

use on the District Line's extension to Upminster. The excuse given at the time was 'the difficulty of obtaining new rails' in the hard-pressed post-war era but I'm sure the decision had already been made. The remaining conductor rails were removed in 1955 having never been used.

Its anachronistic country railway character was captured in a lyrical aricle by H.W.A. Linecar in the March 1951 issue of *Trains Illustrated* magazine. Highgate station is described as 'a curious architectural mixture of concrete and antique woodwork, bounded on three sides by high wooded banks, out of which the tunnel shell of a yet uncompleted escalator to the railway projects like the muzzle of a Wellesian space-gun.

'The push-and-pull train snorts into another short snug tunnel at the end of the platform and emerges at the top of its climb alongside Highgate Wood. A few yards north of the tunnel it rattles over the points of Park Junction and begins its run along the Alexandra Palace branch proper.

'Cranley Gardens station is situated at the north-east corner of Highgate Wood. Here trees and flowerbeds line the platforms and though the track may boast some rusty electric rails and though power cables may sneak along under the platform walls, the station is lit by gas lamps, typical of a country station.

'The train rumbles along behind trim gardens to Muswell Hill. Here the stationmaster from Cranley Gardens, who whistled the train away from the previous station, now alights from it and prepares to do the same duty here.'

The poetic Mr Linecar described Alexandra Palace station as 'dark and cavernous, still retaining the air of the more dilapidated country terminus.' His final image is poignant and prescient: 'the signalman, drowsing in his paint-scaled box, listens stolidly and with caution to every new rumour about the future advent of electric trains.'

Complete closure soon followed the abandonment of the electrification scheme. The last train, composed of eight gas-lit coaches hauled by a tank engine (this at the dawn of the nuclear age!), ran on the afternoon of 3rd July 1954 and distinguished itself by breaking down at Highgate, having to be rescued by the locomotive of a following goods train. The return trip arrived back at Finsbury Park 35 minutes late. It seemed somehow appropriate.

A rearguard action to keep the line on was mounted by an organisation called the North London Passengers Protection Association Limited. This had grand plans to reopen the line and operate it using ex-GWR diesel railcars acquired through hire purchase, known as 'the never-never' in those pre-credit card days. The association claimed that the staff needed to operate the service would be negligible. There would be no ticket offices, just a conductor and driver for each train – an idea that was later taken up on branch lines all over the country. Regular passengers could become shareholders and have the benefit of reduced fares and any profits would be ploughed back to improve the service.

The association's secretary, Mr Thomas Herbert, told the newspapers that they were 'confident we can squash any objections London Transport may have. Any inquiry would show that the repacement bus services are inadequate. Men are bringing out their cars and motor-cycles, adding to the traffic

124

congestion. I don't see how the Minister of Transport can refuse to let us reopen the line. It is a national asset that is going begging.'

Brave and prophetic words but sadly nothing came of a scheme that would have been by four years the first standard gauge preserved line in Britain.

Freight working between Finsbury Park and Edgware or High Barnet ended in 1964 and after that the only use of the route was for the occasional movement of tube cars between the LT Northern Line depot at Highgate and Drayton Park, on the Northern's Moorgate line. As the tracks were not electrified the trains had to be hauled by battery-operated locomotives. This ceased in 1970 and the following year the rails between Finsbury Park and Highgate were removed, the track onwards to the Palace having gone several years before.

# The Parkland Walk

Unlike most of the 'lost lines' in this book, the majority of the route can be easily explored on foot as it has been converted into a footpath, known as the Parkland Walk. After crossing the main line north of Finsbury Park station, the path runs north-west on a slight embankment towards Stroud Green station. The houses, in Florence Road and Lancaster Road on either side of the line, are tall Victorian and Edwardian buildings of great character. There are no traces of the platforms or any trackside buildings at Stroud Green but the station house still stands proudly at street level next to the bridge.

The footpath then crosses over the Gospel Oak to Barking line and continues westwards to Crouch End. The road bridge over Mount Pleasant Villas was the scene of death and destruction on one never-to-be-forgotten night in the early 1980s. Fire engines attended the scene as both road and rail vehicles were ablaze. A railway wagon lay on its side under the bridge and was still there the next day. No real disaster though – just the shooting of a Greater London Council propaganda film about the dangers of transporting nuclear waste by rail!

The approach to Crouch End station is through a leafy cutting with brick arched retaining walls, hideously scarred by brightly-

*Stapleton Hall Road, c1910. Looking towards Stroud Green Road, the station is on the right. (Dick Whetstone, Hornsey Historical Society)*

*The Parkland Walk between Stroud Green and Crouch End stations, looking north-west towards Crouch End. (Author)*

coloured modern graffiti. A burnt out motor bike lies between the platforms, which still survive almost intact, and just beyond the station I found a rusty old safe lying on the track. Were these remains of a safe-cracking job that failed, and did the safe still have the gold inside, I wondered? Probably not.

The station building was on the bridge that crosses the track but has long since been demolished. A shop and a café that stood to one side of it are still there though. I don't suppose the café gets many rail travellers as customers nowadays.

The Parkland Walk is noted for its flora and fauna. Habitats are protected and species conserved. Perhaps the most unusual mammal noted is the Chinese Muntjac, a small type of deer occasionally seen on the more secluded parts of the walk by those quiet, patient or lucky enough. This species, an introduction, is believed to be extending its range southwards from breeding populations in the south of Hertfordshire.

We are lucky to have this green oasis. In the mid 1980s the Department of Transport's East London Assessment Study, noting a linear strip of open land that did not seem to be doing anything useful, proposed constructing a six-lane motorway along it. The residents and local societies who had fought to get the park in the first place were soon up in arms as the 'Save the Parkland Walk' campaign group. The planners backed down, agreeing that the proposals would have 'unacceptable environmental consequences'. That is until the next time some bright bureaucrat fills a few idle moments by drawing some lines on a map!

Entering a shady cutting the path heads towards Highgate station preceded by the two-bore tunnel under Highgate Hill. There are gates across the entrances to the twin single-track tunnels but they are not locked and it looks possible to walk through to the remains of Highgate station, but I would not recommend it. You enter at your own risk and the slightly sinister groups of youths that I encountered near the entrance were enough to deter me from entering alone.

The official Parkland Walk takes an attractive detour through Highgate Woods to rejoin the Palace branch near the site of Cranley Gardens station. However, it is still possible to see the cutting and site of the former surface station at Highgate by

*Safe but not sound at Crouch End! (Author)*

*Entrance to Highgate South tunnels seen from the Crouch End direction.*
*Highgate station lies just beyond. Entering the tunnels is not recommended!*
*(Author)*

walking a short distance along the Archway Road to the
Northern Line tube station.

Highgate station is rather odd. The Northern Line platforms
are underground, more or less below the trackbed of the Great
Northern Railway whose surface route it takes over half a mile to
the north, continuing to Finchley Central, High Barnet or Mill
Hill East. The buildings of the surface station are largely
complete, though derelict, and can be glimpsed through the
trees from the footpaths leading down to the entrances to the
tube station. It had been largely rebuilt in 1940-1 to the designs of
Charles Holden, the architect responsible for many of the
innovative new stations built, particularly on the Piccadilly Line
extensions in the 1930s. There had even been plans for a
decorative weather-vane featuring Dick Whittington and his cat,
whose hearing of the bells of the City from Highgate Hill
features in so many pantomimes.

These remains of the rebuilt surface platforms lie forlorn in a deep cutting hidden from the busy Archway Road. There was a central island platform with tracks on either side and the passageways linking these platforms with the tube station still exist although closed off. How close this station came to being part of the London Transport network is shown by the impression of the well-known LT roundel station name sign on one of the walls, visible even now. The tunnels on either side of the station are still there and in places still bear the cable brackets for the London Transport electrification scheme which never came. The northbound tunnel, north of Highgate station, received a direct hit from a bomb during the Blitz and the rebuilding work needed is still very evident in the brickwork of the portal.

North of the tunnel, in the fork between the Edgware/Barnet and Alexandra Palace lines, were Wellington Sidings. It was here that that the Royal Train was stabled by the LNER when not in service. When the depot was taken over by the Underground, the London Passenger Transport Board had to pay for a replacement building to be put up alongside the LNER main line at Wood Green.

To rejoin the Parkland Walk you have to turn down Muswell Hill, passing on the right the house where the comedian Peter Sellers lived from 1936 to 1940. A blue plaque recording this has been placed there. From his bedroom window the youngster could probably see the radio and television masts at Alexandra Palace. Did he ever realise, I wonder, how much the BBC, who used the building in those days, would feature in his life?

An impressive terrace of shops gives the clue to the location of Cranley Gardens station and here the formation of the Alexandra Palace branch, now the Parkland Walk, can be rejoined. A garden centre that must be sited on the former station yard has a fence made up of old railway sleepers next to the footpath; presumably they were salvaged when the railway track was lifted. Further on there is an impressive view over Muswell Hill from the bridge over St James's Lane. Beyond this the old railway viaduct gives an even more extensive prospect south-eastwards across London. All the major landmarks can be seen but you need a good head for heights and children should not be encouraged to lean over the railings. More timid souls might prefer to keep back or towards the other side of the viaduct where the prospect is not so alarming! Below the railway the seventeen arches are home to various car-repair firms, furniture restorers and the like.

At Muswell Hill the Parkland Walk leaves the old railway once again and its route is more difficult to see. A curious sign on the fence warns that this is the 'Muswell Hill School Dog Parking Area'. It goes on to exhort parents to 'please leave your dogs here for their safety and that of the children'. One wonders who is deemed to be in the greater danger! But it is only a short walk to the still-impressive Palace, set in its attractive park. The buildings of the branch terminus were still in place in August 2000 but are now swamped by recent commercial development and the site is inaccessible.

Alexandra Palace is now styled the 'Alexandra Palace

*Muswell Hill viaduct, view southwards from St James' Lane, c1880. (Hornsey Historical Society)*

Complex' as if a mere Palace was not enough and boasts a Palm Court Suite, Exhibition Centre and other attractions. What is still free though is the view to the south, one of the finest in London.

There could yet be another twist in this tale. Trains might one day run again along this long-abandoned route. Following in the footsteps of the North London Passengers Protection Association, the Muswell Hill Metro Group has ambitious plans for a light-rail electric tramway with services every ten minutes between Finsbury Park and Alexandra Palace. Up to 2,000 people every half hour could go to and from events at Alexandra Palace without clogging up local roads. The trams would run alongside the Parkland Walk, which would be upgraded and landscaped, preserving a green corridor which is valued by local people. Something similar happens at Bitton station on the outskirts of Bristol where the restored railway shares its cutting with the Avon Valley Cycleway. However, although the group has been campaigning for many years, they are yet to convince the London Borough of Haringey that the scheme is viable or desirable.

# An electric pioneer

As well as being served by two branch railways – the GER Palace Gates branch we shall come to later – Alexandra Palace was also the destination of London's first electric tramway. Like the Palace itself and the railways, the tramway did not live up to the optimistic hopes of its promoters.

In this case the optimistic entrepreneur was a Mr Thomas John Hawkins of Ashford, Middlesex. Described as 'a former horticultural builder', Mr Hawkins had run an amusement park at Wembley in the summer of 1897. He must have made a profit on this because, undeterred by the failure of previous owners of Alexandra Palace, he took on North London's White Elephant, opening it up once more at Easter 1898 with a range of well-publicised attractions which included 'Balloon Ascents, Military Bands, Tournaments, Boating, A Maze, Bicycle Polo and Fireworks'.

To make it easier to get people up the hill to Alexandra Park to enjoy all this, Mr Hawkins proposed an electric tramway from the Wood Green Gate on the eastern boundary of the park, a 600 yard long route of double track, climbing 130 ft and with a semi-circular run-round loop at the top. He went into partnership with the spectacularly-named Elektrizitatsgesellschaft Wandruszka of Berlin, who saw this project as an opportunity to demonstrate the new technology of electric traction to the transport authorities in London.

The park opened for the new season on 8th April 1898 but the tramway was not able to be opened until the somewhat unpropitious date of Friday 13th May. Four single-deck tramcars, drawing their power from overhead wires supported by poles between the two tracks, provided a much easier way for the visitors to reach the myriad attractions at the top of the hill.

Things did not go entirely to plan, however. Descending tramcars were found to be liable to skid in wet weather and a fully-laden car was involved in an accident on 30th May. Three people were injured and were later awarded damages against the proprietors. It was hastily decided to suspend operation of the tramway in inclement weather – just the days when its services would be most appreciated, of course. In June a fitter employed by the German manufacturers was killed when he struck his head on one of the trolley-poles while attempting to leap off a moving tram. Things were not going too well!

Moreover, there were complaints about the cost of the service: 'It is a generally expressed opinion that 2d is too much for a ride up the hill from Wood Green to Alexandra Palace in the new electric tramcar,' the local paper reported. 'The distance is comparatively slight compared with the pennyworth from the Archway Tavern to the top of Highgate Hill. It is nothing like the value for money you get in twopenny rides along Southend Pier.'

The fare was reduced to one penny in 1899 but the new season was a disaster. The number of visitors to the park dropped, bad weather and a lack of attractions being blamed. The park and the tramway closed at the end of September and the trams never ran again. Hawkins went bankrupt and the tramway was dis-mantled before the end of the year. The four tramcars eventually found a new home with the Great Grimsby Street Tramways

Company where they were reconstructed as double-deckers and came into service in 1902.

It was perhaps all done rather too hastily. Later owners of Alexandra Palace recognised the need for a tramway up to the top. By 1905 there was a line up from Muswell Hill and in 1906 a completely new tramway was opened on the route of Hawkins's line. These remained in service until replaced by buses in 1938.

Buses still climb up the steep road from Wood Green to the Palace but very few of their passengers are aware that they are following the course of London's first electric tramway. Certainly there are no structures or relics to be seen today.

# To the Palace Gates by GER

The Great Eastern Railway was also keen to share in the jamboree promised by the Alexandra Palace scheme and in 1878 opened a two and a half mile branch from Seven Sisters station on its Enfield Town branch to what was somewhat misleadingly known as Palace Gates station, very close to the Wood Green station on the GNR main line. Actually any hot and harassed family, loaded with picnic and other impedimenta essential for a good day out, would have been not best pleased to discover on leaving the station that a further three-quarters of a mile uphill walk awaited them before they reached their destination.

This disadvantage was perhaps hinted at, though, in an otherwise glowing testimonial to the new line published in a local newspaper of the day which I found among the Haringey Borough archives at the Bruce Castle Museum in Tottenham: 'At the terminus at Wood Green called Palace Gates is one of the most convenient stations to be seen on any line around London. The awning covers a greater part of the carriages enabling persons to enter or leave them without the possibility of getting wet. Passengers can join the trams in the wettest weather with an equal immunity to damp clothes.' Clearly the intemperate climate of North London was a matter of pressing concern to the Victorians!

'The waiting rooms are commodious,' the newspaper in-

GREAT EASTERN RAILWAY.

OPENING

OF THE

ALEXANDRA PARK BRANCH,

1st JANUARY, 1878.

Trains will run from Liverpool Street

TO THE

GREEN LANES STATION,

WOOD GREEN,

Calling at intermediate Stations, on Week Days, at 7.40, 8.10, 8.55, 9.10, and 9.58 a.m.; and every Half-hour from 10.40 a.m. to 9.40 p.m., and at 10.20, 11.0, and 11.40 p.m.;

AND FROM THE GREEN LANES STATION

Every Half-hour, 7.6 a.m. to 9.6 p.m.; and at 9.46, 10.26, and 11.6 p.m.

ON SUNDAYS.

From LIVERPOOL STREET.—Every 40 minutes, leaving Liverpool Street at 9.15, 9.55, and 10.35 a.m., and 1.15, 1.55, 2.35, 3.15, 3.55, 4.35, 5.15, 5.55, 6.35, 7.15, 7.55, 8.35, 9.15, 9.55, and 10.35 p.m.

From GREEN LANES.—Every 40 minutes, leaving Green Lanes at 8.41, 9.21, and 10.1 a.m., and 12.41, 1.21, 2.1, 2.41, 3.21, 4.1, 4.41, 5.21, 6.1, 6.41, 7.21, 8.1, 8.41, 9.21, and 10.1 p.m.

The GREEN LANES STATION is only a short distance from the WOOD GREEN ENTRANCE to the Alexandra Park.

Passengers from and to the Enfield Branch Stations to and from the Alexandra Park, change Trains at the Seven Sisters Station.

S. SWARBRICK,

London, Dec. 1877.                General Manager.

Waterow & Sons Limited, Printers, London Wall, London.

GREAT EASTERN RAILWAY.

ALEXANDRA PARK BRANCH.

OPENING

OF THE

PALACE GATES STATION.

The Palace Gates Station, situate close to the Alexandra Park, will be OPENED FOR TRAFFIC on MONDAY, 7th OCTOBER, 1878, and the Trains now running between Liverpool Street and the Green Lanes Station, will run to and from the Palace Gates Station.

The Trains will start from the Palace Gates Station for Liverpool Street, on Week Days, every Half Hour from 8.35 a.m. to 9.5 p.m., and at 7.5, 7.35, and 8.1 a.m., and 9.42, 10.25, and 11.5 p.m. On Sundays, every Half Hour from 8.35 to 10.5 a.m., and 12.35 to 10.5 p.m.

S. SWARBRICK,

London, October, 1878.                General Manager.

PRINTED AT THE COMPANY'S WORKS, STRATFORD.

*Notices advertising the opening of the Alexandra Park Branch, January 1878, and the Palace Gates Station in October 1878. (Courtesy of Bruce Castle Museum, Haringey Council)*

formed its readers, 'and will be fitted with great taste. The new line will doubtless be largely patronised by the inhabitants of the localities through which it runs. The entire absence of tunnels is alone a recommendation in its favour and the route is marked by many other pleasant features. The manner in which the railway has been constructed reflects much credit upon the engineers and the contractor. The line presents a very neat and substantial appearance and the works are pronounced by those competent to judge as being of superior character throughout.'

The line curved away to the west from the country end of Seven Sisters station and climbed quite steeply north-westwards via Green Lanes (later Noel Park) station to the terminus, seven miles from Liverpool Street. The impressively laid-out terminus was built as a through station as there were somewhat

*Seven Sisters station, looking north (GER, c1910s). The Palace Gates branch can be seen curving off to the left. (Lens of Sutton)*

improbable plans to link up with the GNR branch at Alexandra Palace, a route which would have needed some heavy and expensive engineering!

As with the GNR branch, the Palace's failure as a leisure attraction meant that the Palace Gates line did not begin to pay its way until the adjoining fields began to be sold off for building towards the end of the 19th century. An intensive suburban service developed, trains running not only to Liverpool Street but also to North Woolwich. This was much appreciated by local men working in the docks or at the massive GER engineering works at Stratford.

Once again the development of competing tram and bus services damaged the revenues of the branch. In 1932 the opening of the Piccadilly Line from Finsbury Park through Turnpike Lane, Wood Green and Bounds Green was another blow as these stations were very close to Noel Park and Palace Gates and offered a quicker and more convenient route to the City and West End. Even so the LNER (which had by now taken over the line) was confident enough to announce a rebuilding of

136

Noel Park station, although little had been done before work was curtailed at the start of the Second World War.

Just before the Second World War a link was constructed between the Palace Gates goods yard and the nearby GNR main line at Bounds Green. This enabled suburban carriages to be taken to a washing plant at the new Bounds Green depot and was also used by some excursion trains to the east coast from GNR suburban stations in the doom-laden summer of 1939. In 1944 a connection was established with the ex-GER Hertford loop at Bowes Park, enabling wartime freight movements between Peterborough and the marshalling yard at Temple Mills, Leyton. In the 1950s this was used by excursions to Clacton and Southend. Other excursions down the line included Sunday School treats run from Palace Gates to various destinations.

The war, though, led to severe reductions in the service on the Palace Gates branch from which it never really recovered despite the optimism of G.H. Lake in his book, *The Railways of Tottenham*, published in 1946. Mr Lake wrote of the branch that 'all the stations reflect the heavy passenger traffic of bygone days but with conversion to electric working in days to come they will no doubt regain their former activity.'

But with the frequent trams and trolleybuses and the faster service offered by the Piccadilly tube, perhaps the Palace Gates branch just was not convenient enough any more. Even Mr Lake noted that 'at Seven Sisters station the Palace Gates line suffers from the long walk necessary to reach the branch platforms from the main booking office in West Green Road. To help passengers who live on the Seven Sisters side of the station a small booking office is available. This however is now open only in the early mornings and, when it is closed, persons on that side of the station wishing to travel to Palace Gates have to walk right round the station site, a considerable distance, and then make their way back to the platform by a long footpath.' Having come out of Seven Sisters station by the wrong exit on my first visit, I can vouch for the fact that it takes quite a time to walk from one side of the station to the other.

This lack of consideration of the needs of passengers was repeated in many suburban stations in those days and was a factor in the old-fashioned steam-hauled services losing out to more modern means of transport wherever there was a choice.

In September 1958 there was brief flurry of excitement when British Railways put on in the Noel Park Goods Depot in Pelham Road 'An Exhibition of Locomotives, Carriages, Wagons and Containers and a Demonstration of Mechanical Appliances'. This was in connection with the Borough of Wood Green Charter Celebrations. Among the exhibits was the A4 Pacific *Mallard*, the holder of the record speed for a steam engine, 126 mph, set in 1938. That such a star should be seen on the humble Palace Gates branch was quite a coup. I suspect that she would have been moved down from the main line at Bounds Green over the link constructed before the war, rather than from the Seven Sisters direction.

By 1962 the by now restricted service to Palace Gates was the last outpost of steam on the old GER suburban network in London. Diesel multiple units briefly ran a more intensive service, perhaps in an attempt to revitalise the line, or possibly for driver training, but in 1963 the North Woolwich service was cut back to operate from Tottenham Hale and the Palace Gates branch was no more.

One local resident recalled the last day: 'My son and I went on a train to North Woolwich, crossing on the Free Ferry to Woolwich. We returned on the very last train to Palace Gates on a day when snow covered the ground. There were queues at the booking office, not people travelling but to buy tickets on the last day of operation.'

Unlike the GNR line from Highgate, transformed into the Parkland Walk, it is not easy to explore the Palace Gates route on foot. Socially too, it is very different. The upper middle-class streets of Highgate and Muswell Hill give way to a teeming cosmopolitan area that slides imperceptibly from Wood Green to Tottenham.

# On foot from Palace Gates

Tracing the route it is much easier to walk down from Alexandra Palace to Wood Green than to climb the other way. The extensive views across London are in front of you as you come down.

Wood Green main line station has in recent years been somewhat optimistically renamed Alexandra Palace, in defiance of the Trades Descriptions Act!

The route of the northern extension of the Palace Gates branch round to Bounds Green is strongly fenced off and leads to the modern GNER carriage sheds. The site of Palace Gates station is just beyond, behind a quiet little group of roads by the Avenue Gardens. The imposing red-brick station buildings were demolished some time in the 1970s. The platforms themselves, heavily overgrown, lasted into the 1980s. A sheltered housing development overlooking a broad strip of grassland marks the spot and a short stretch of embankment leads to the abutments of a demolished bridge over Park Avenue. Beyond, the route is hidden behind houses and obliterated by the massive new shopping developments of Wood Green.

The Argos Superstore, part of the wonderfully-named 'Wood Green Shopping City', is where Noel Park station used to be. The station building survived in commercial use into the 1970s, latterly as Noel Park Distributors Ltd., the railway viaduct still towering over the undistinguished 1930s building, but all traces went when the area was redeveloped. Not quite all though! Tucked away down Gladstone Mews and Pelham Road the original Great Eastern Railway Goods Office building, a narrow two-storey brick structure, still survives.

Close inspection of the street map gives the game away. Westbury Road, running north-east from Turnpike Lane tube station, rises to cross the trackbed whose line can be traced in a strip of allotments next to Mannock Road. The Belmont Road bridge survives more or less unaltered. Part of the trackbed and the site of the goods yard are now occupied by Langham School (formerly the William Foster's School) and its tennis courts. This is, of course, securely fenced but a good view of the bridge can be seen from Downhills Park Recreation Ground. Further on, the positioning of modern buildings north of West Green Road, and visible from it, reflects the rail alignment.

West Green station was here, at the junction with Philip Lane. A low range of derelict premises (until recently a car-hire business) on the north side of the road, boarded up after a bad fire in June 2001, is all that is left, apart from a bridge parapet at

*Belmont Road bridge over the former Palace Gates branch. View from Downhills Recreation Ground. (Author)*

an angle on the opposite site of the road. Although the station buildings, increasingly vandalised, lasted through much of the 1960s there is nothing left now. From here, almost all the way to Seven Sisters, the trackbed has been used for a line of new housing developments. Someone with a sense of local transport history was responsible for naming the first of these Gresley Close, after the famous locomotive engineer of the LNER, but perhaps Brunel Close off Kirkton Road is less appropriate. Wood Green is hardly in Great Western territory.

The humps of former bridges over the railway can be seen in Cornwall Road and Avenue Road. Part of the trackbed here is also used as allotments. At Seven Sisters all that remains of the erstwhile GER Palace Gates branch is the earthworks of the truncated spur, fenced off from a children's playground. Beyond the station, which is still used by suburban trains running between Liverpool Street and Enfield, there is a connection to the Gospel Oak–Barking line (which still has quite a frequent passenger service) and this spur is occasionally used by goods trains. The journey from Gospel Oak to Barking, like the better-known North London line from Richmond to North Woolwich, provides excellent opportunities for views of the various railways radiating out northwards from London and is recommended to those wishing to capture something of the atmosphere of the forgotten suburban railways of North and East London.

One ambitious scheme, proposed by Mr Lake in 1946, was to resite Seven Sisters station slightly to the south, at the junction with the spur towards Barking and combining it with South Tottenham station on the Barking line (whose services in those days ran to Kentish Town rather than Gospel Oak).

Just to the west was the relatively short-lived station at St Ann's Road (at the junction with the Seven Sisters Road). The optimism and excitement which greeted the opening of this station in 1882 is captured in a report in the *Tottenham & Edmonton Weekly Herald* on 6th October 1882:

'On Monday morning last the new station on the Tottenham & Hampstead Junction Railway erected for the accommodation of the large and increasing district of St Ann's was opened for public traffic. Originally it was intended that the opening should

141

take place on 1st June last but unavoidable delays prevented this arrangement being carried out. All trains from South Tottenham to Moorgate Street will now stop at the new station which will be a boon to the neighbourhood as hitherto travellers from St Ann's Road had to go to either Stamford Hill or Seven Sisters stations on the Great Eastern system.

'The opening was regarded with great satisfaction, flags of all nations supplied by Messrs. Eveniss and Pike, proprietors of the Victoria Tavern, St Ann's Road, were suspended from one side of the road to the other and various tradesmen met to congratulate themselves on the long deferred benefit having come at last. There is no doubt that the new station will largely add to the prosperity of the St Ann's district by bringing to it a considerable number of additional residents, the want of proper railway accommodation having hitherto been a great drawback.

'On Monday evening there was a brilliant display of fireworks from an elevated position on the Victoria Tavern. A large crowd assembled but everything passed off without a hitch of any kind.'

I doubt whether such festivity would accompany the opening of a new station these days – perhaps a junior transport minister unveiling a plaque on the wall of a basic and supposedly vandal-proof unstaffed platform shelter would be the best one could hope for.

The end of St Ann's Road came as a sad contrast to the high jinks which marked its opening. It was really too close to South Tottenham and to Seven Sisters to be of great importance and the station closed as an economy measure during the Second World War and never reopened. 'How different was the closing,' wrote Mr Lake. 'Not a protest or even a sigh of regret. The booking office doors just closed for the last time and, next day, a disinterested public passed by quite oblivious to the fact that almost exactly sixty years earlier those same doors had opened to the accompaniment of fireworks.'

Today almost none of the local people will know that there was ever a station there at all.

# 12
# Taking The Pig To Edgware

## *Finsbury Park to Edgware ... and beyond*

*GNR steam railcar providing the Edgware branch service at Finchley (Church End), now Finchley Central. (Lens of Sutton)*

Like Uxbridge, the town of Edgware saw its fortunes decline in the first half of the 19th century as the coaching trade, on which it has prospered, wilted in the face of competition from the new-fangled railway. It was not until August 1867 that the independently-promoted Edgware, Highgate and London Railway was opened from Seven Sisters Road (now Finsbury Park) to Edgware with intermediate stations at Crouch End, Highgate, East End Finchley (later known as East Finchley), Finchley & Hendon (now Finchley Central) and Mill Hill (now Mill Hill East).

In 1872 a 4 mile branch to High Barnet was opened and in 1873 the branch from Highgate to Alexandra Palace, which has already been described in detail (in Chapter 11), as well as the section from Finsbury Park.

The layout of the junction at Finchley Central to this day still makes it quite clear that the Edgware line came first and that the Barnet route was a branch of it, but very quickly the Edgware line became the poor relation. Suburban development took place along the Barnet and Palace routes eventually but the single-track to Edgware seemed to make very little difference. It even acquired a dubious bucolic nickname, 'The Pig'. However, the opening of the North Middlesex Gas Works near Mill Hill station in 1886 and an army barracks and depot nearby in 1906 helped increase goods traffic.

In June 1906, in an attempt to steal some traffic from the

*Mill Hill East in LNER days; view towards London. Note 'For Mill Hill Barracks' on the station sign. Northern Line trains still depart from here but the line to Edgware is no more. The station itself is little changed today. (Lens of Sutton)*

144

Midland main line station at Mill Hill, the Great Northern, who had now acquired the branch, opened a wooden halt, The Hale, just west of where the Midland line crossed above the branch. It had very little effect.

When Edgware did begin to grow it was as a result of housing developments stimulated by the arrival of the London Underground line northwards from Golders Green in 1924. This benefited the freight receipts – the yard at the branch terminus was extended to cope with the extra traffic in building materials and domestic fuels – but the new residents preferred to use the tube to get to London instead of the rather devious route from Edgware via Highgate and Finsbury Park. It did not help that there were very few through trains, passengers usually having to change at Finchley.

The annual Royal Air Force displays at Hendon aerodrome in the 1930s, however, always brought more passengers than this

*Mill Hill (The Hale), close to the point where the Mill Hill East–Edgware branch passed under the Midland main line. (Lens of Sutton)*

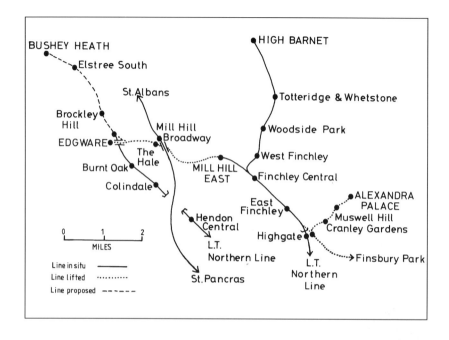

already antiquated branch could cope with. Trains would run every few minutes to the little platform at The Hale (by now renamed 'Mill Hill for The Hale'). The trains would then be parked end to end along the single track to Edgware until it was time to take the crowds back again. The few regulars on the line could not have been too happy about the disruption!

By now plans were afoot to incorporate the High Barnet, Edgware via Mill Hill and Alexandra Palace lines into the London Underground network under the so-called 'Northern Heights' proposals. As far as the Edgware branch was concerned the plan was to double the existing single line, divert the line into the existing Edgware station on the tube line from Golders Green, and to extend it to Bushey Heath with intermediate stations at Brockley Hill and Elstree South where it was expected housing development would follow as it had done elsewhere. From being an insignificant halt, The Hale would have become a major interchange, a joint station serving both the new route and the LMS main line trains.

146

A large new depot was to be built at Aldenham as the cramped facilities at Golders Green could not have coped with all the extra trains required and Edgware station would have been completely rebuilt to allow trains to run through. Bushey Heath station would have been at the junction of Elstree Road and the Watford bypass. It was planned to be the focal point of a new shopping centre with cinema and pub. The design would have been similar to the contemporary station at Cockfosters at the northern end of the Piccadilly Line.

Work began on the new scheme – the main depot buildings were constructed and equipped first as it was suspected that they could be vital for the forthcoming war effort (in fact they were adapted to become part of an aircraft factory constructing Halifax bombers).

To allow all this to happen, the Edgware branch service was replaced by a 'railway bus' service in September 1939. Other

*Mill Hill (The Hale). Midland Railway main line crossing the Edgware branch in background. (Lens of Sutton)*

147

matters were preoccupying most people by then, of course, but the relative quiet of the 'phony war' period at that time enabled work to proceed. North of Edgware, it had not progressed very far but the partly built tunnels under Brockley Hill found a use as an army firing range. High Barnet got its new electric trains in 1940. The Edgware branch was reopened as far as what was by now known as Mill Hill East in May 1941, largely to improve transport links to the military barracks. The track had been doubled by then but in fact only one line was used by the new trains and the other was soon removed again. The 'railway bus' to Edgware was withdrawn but railway tickets were now valid on the normal bus services.

Steam-hauled goods trains continued to run – an odd sight amid the intensive tube service – but to get these trains beyond Mill Hill East posed difficulties as there was no adequate signalling in place. Derailments sometimes occurred and the guard would have to return to Finchley Central by bus to summon assistance.

After the war nothing came of the ambitious plans for tube trains to Edgware via Mill Hill East and on to Bushey Heath. Some preliminary work had been done, however. It had been intended to completely rebuild Mill Hill (The Hale) and parts of the old wooden platforms were replaced. Beyond Edgware, the viaduct that would have carried Brockley Hill station was partially completed – a series of six round-headed arches but little more that stood forlornly in a field until the late 1950s. The line would have passed under Brockley Hill in twin-bore tunnels like at Highgate (Chapter 11) and work was started on these as well. After the war the new government's Green Belt proposals meant that no significant housing development would be allowed along this route. Rather oddly, however, railway tickets continued to be valid for travel on local buses from Mill Hill East to The Hale and Edgware until the late 1960s – even season tickets were issued. In fact, until 7th September 1969 you could buy from the British Railways booking office at Mill Hill Broadway London Transport tickets showing the issuing station as 'Mill Hill The Hale' and valid on the 240 bus route. It was as if the electrification scheme had happened after all!

Goods trains did continue to run from Mill Hill East to

Edgware until 1964 but the passenger service was never restored. This left the stub end from Finchley Central to Mill Hill East as a quirky little appendix whose existence on the Underground map must puzzle many.

Visitors arriving by train at Mill Hill East will see a short section of line beyond the front of the train but this leads nowhere. The trackbed is blocked by more recent development but can be found again by turning left out of the station and then left again down Sanders Lane. The bridge taking the lane across the trackbed is still in place and there is a footpath that goes under the bridge and leading towards The Hale.

This path is signposted 'Barnet Countryside Walks' and can be followed easily for about a mile. It runs between banks and trees with sports fields on either side. The concrete posts put in during the war for the electrification are still there and most of them still bear the metal brackets to hold the lineside cables.

This path comes to an end at Page Street and it is then necessary to follow Bunns Lane under the A1 Barnet bypass, the

*Sanders Lane bridge crosses the Edgware line just north of its present terminus at Mill Hill East. (Author)*

149

M1 and the main line through Mill Hill Broadway to Lyndhurst Park. Here, at the site of The Hale, the Bunns Lane bridge still exists but its arches are bricked up. There is no sign of the little halt, however. The branch line then ran along the park boundary and can be traced as a line of trees and impenetrable undergrowth towards Hale Lane where it ran behind the back gardens.

The route can be clearly seen as a wooded cutting where it reaches Deans Lane but it is securely fenced and gated and inaccessible. On the other side of the road it disappears into London Transport property, leading to Edgware Depot. The last part of the trackbed approaching Edgware station is used as sidings to accommodate Northern Line trains. Between the tube platforms and the bus station is the space where the platforms for the service onwards to Bushey Heath would have been but for the post-war changes in planning policy.

Beyond, the arches at Brockley Hill were partially demolished in 1958. Only the lower sections survive now and can be seen to

*The Northern Line terminus at Edgware in early London Transport days. (Stations UK)*

the north of Edgware Way. The tunnels under Brockley Hill were used as a rifle range for a while but were bricked up in 1953 and there is nothing left to see. The depot at Aldenham, used for aircraft construction during the war, became a bus-repair works afterwards but has since been closed and demolished.

In 1995 site clearance work south-east of Edgware station revealed relics of this long-abandoned project that had been previously obscured by foliage. These included the bridge abutments that once supported a plate girder bridge built to carry northbound Northern Line trains to Bushey Heath over a new alignment for the Golders Green services. Because of the abandonment of the Bushey Heath scheme this bridge was never used although it had remained in place into the 1960s. The abutments can be seen from passing trains, as can the short stretch of the old line back towards Mill Hill.

# 13
# Enfield Oddments

*Goods trains in general*
*The Churchbury Loop*
*Angel Road to Lower Edmonton*
*Wood Green to Enfield*

*Hanging out the washing at Forty Hill station, c1936. (Enfield Council Local History Unit)*

## Goods trains in general

The surviving railways of Middlesex are almost exclusively passenger-carrying operations now but in the past freight traffic sustained many of our lost lines for much of their existence and

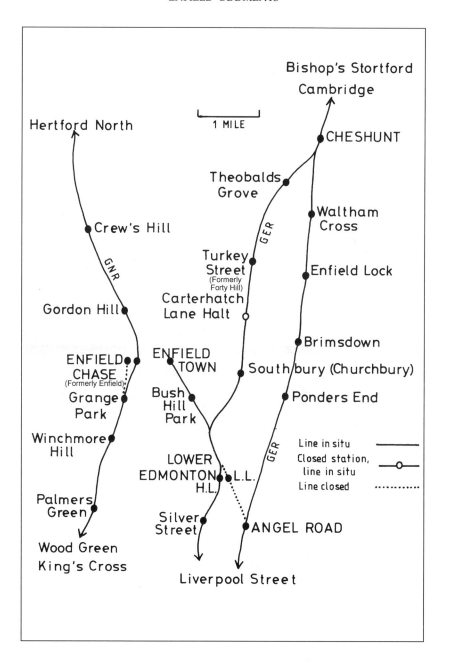

153

in some cases, such as the Staines West and Brentford lines, they have kept at least part of their routes in operation long after the passenger services ceased running. On most of the working lines in the county goods traffic is but a distant memory and slow-moving goods trains would not fit easily into an intensive commuter service.

But it was not always so. Many lines in their early days carried the materials for the houses that were to become the new homes of their future passengers. In 1931, for example, there was enough housebuilding going on in Shepperton to justify building a special siding on the approach to the station for materials being brought in for a local building firm, W.J. Lavender.

For many years until May 1965 the same branch saw unlikely, but presumably lucrative, traffic to the yard at Hampton, in the gruesome form of frozen horseflesh for a local pet food manufacturer. This came all the way from the bleak plains of Central Europe in refrigerated wagons belonging to the Hungarian State Railways, an unlikely sight in the equally flat land of West Middlesex!

Until the 1950s most suburban stations along the lines radiating out through Middlesex had their own goods yard. Domestic coal was the most usual commodity carried and from these local yards the coal merchants' lorries or horses and carts would set off around the local streets in those pre-smokeless days. In later years many of these small local yards were closed and coal was distributed by road from larger concentration depots such as the one built in the old station yard at Enfield Chase in 1962. Rail hopper wagons discharged about 59,000 tons of coal a year to lorries waiting below them. These lorries then clogged up the local streets taking the coal to the old yards where the local coal merchants were still based. One wonders whether this was really all that much of an improvement but in any case this change was short-lived as solid fuels began to lose out to electricity, 'clean simplicity' as the advertising slogan had it, or oil-fired central heating. The distribution of oil followed a similar pattern.

Coal in larger quantities was ferried to power stations and gasworks. The Hampton Court Gas Company, for example, had its works next to the railway between Teddington and Hampton

*Forty Hill (Turkey Street) station, 1909. (Enfield Council Local History Unit)*

Wick. The site was not to be redeveloped until the end of the 1990s. Continuing up the line, crossing the River Thames into Surrey, the next station was Kingston where the works belonging to the Kingston Gas Company lay immediately north of the station.

# The Churchbury Loop

Another line that carried a significant amount of freight traffic was the Churchbury Loop between Lower Edmonton on the Great Eastern's Enfield branch and Cheshunt in the Lea Valley. This line has the unusual distinction of being, more than once, 'lost' and then found again, as far as passenger services were concerned.

Opened in 1891 it had substantially-built expensive-looking stations, Churchbury, Forty Hill and Theobalds Grove, set incongruously in empty brickfields and market gardens. Facilities for first class passengers were lavishly provided – somewhat improbably in view of the working-class nature of the district,

155

scattered hamlets inhabited mainly by farm labourers.

It was not a great success. Most journeys to London involved changing at Lower Edmonton, the area was considered unattractive by the well-to-do and it was too far from the City or the West End. Sales of land for building new homes remained sluggish.

But it was the arrival of the Metropolitan Electric Tramways from Lower Edmonton to Enfield Lock and Waltham Cross in 1907 that eventually did for the passenger service. Almost at once passenger receipts (already small) fell by half, more so at Churchbury and Forty Hill, which were nearest to the competition. The GER's proposal in 1909 to withdraw the passenger service created quite a stir. It was unprecedented and the line had the melancholy distinction of being the first in Middlesex to lose its passenger service! Mr Branch, the local MP, tabled a question in the House of Commons for the President of the Board of Trade, a rising young politician named Winston Churchill. He got, of course, the standard politician's answer, to the effect that it was the railway company's business and no concern of the government's. He passed on a letter from the general manager of the Great Eastern Railway which stated that the district had not developed as much as expected and it was all the tramways' fault anyway for pinching the passengers.

The coming of war provided temporary salvation – it's an ill wind that brings nobody any good. From 1915 the Lea Valley became a centre of munitions and related industries, based around Angel Road in Edmonton, at the Royal Gunpowder and Royal Small Arms Factories at Waltham Abbey and Enfield Lock and at the Ponders End Shell Works. These vital establishments needed more labour than could be found in the immediate area and the GER was petitioned to reopen the Churchbury Loop.

This they did, using a steam-operated auto-train with a conductor guard issuing tickets on board to cut station manning costs. They even opened a new station, a basic timber halt in Carterhatch Lane (from which the halt took its name) in June 1916. Much the same thing happened in the Second World War when a new halt named Upper Halliford was provided between Sunbury and Shepperton for the convenience of petrol-rationed war workers at the British Thermostat Factory in Windmill Road.

156

Upper Halliford station survived the end of its war but Carterhatch Lane Halt did not. Neither did the revived Churchbury Loop passenger service, the whole lot closing again at the end of June 1919.

Unlike the Southern Railway, the LNER, which inherited the Churchbury Loop from the GER in the 1923 Grouping of railway companies, did little to promote suburban services. Despite the fact that housing development followed the construction of the Great Cambridge Arterial Road in the 1920s the company resisted the idea of reopening the line to passengers for a second time. Apart from anything else, the Directors of the company pointed out, there was no spare capacity for any more trains to be added to the 58 per hour on the congested tracks between Hackney Downs and Liverpool Street in peak hours.

The stations were mothballed. Forty Hill and Theobalds Grove became private houses and Churchbury station was variously a builder's store and a joinery works. Freight traffic remained steady though, running on one line with the other used to store old wagons. Occasionally there were unexpected bursts of activity when the direct Lea Valley route to Cheshunt was blocked by floods, collision or, in the Second War War, enemy action. In 1928 a bridge under the Lea Valley line at Angel Road collapsed and for several days a passenger service operated once again along the Churchbury Loop. The stations were reopened, their names chalked up on boards, with hurricane lamps the only night-time illumination. The trucks parked on the disused track were hastily moved away and double-track working restored. One wonders what the inhabitants of the former station houses at Forty Hill and Theobalds Grove made of the upheaval.

Double-track working for freight was reintroduced in 1947 but it was something of a surprise to everyone when it was announced that, under the 1954 British Railways Modernisation Plan, the route was to be reopened to passenger traffic. Maybe the lengthy campaign by local people had been heeded, or perhaps the route's value as an alternative to the Lea Valley line had been acknowledged.

Whatever the reason, work to restore the line to main line standards began in 1956. The stations were tastefully refurbished, although not entirely rebuilt as had been at first envisaged. Churchbury station was renamed Southbury, and Forty Hill became Turkey Street after the road it stood in. The first man to be appointed stationmaster at Theobalds Grove was, appropriately, the son of the first booking clerk. The line as a whole was to be in future known as the Southbury Line. There was never any suggestion that Carterhatch Lane Halt (demolished after closure in 1919) should be resurrected and no trace of it remains. The long-awaited passenger service was inaugurated with some ceremony in November 1960.

The freight traffic that kept the line alive during its wilderness years withered away. During the 1960s all the stations saw their goods depots close, the last being Southbury in December 1970. However, the Southbury Line occupies a unique place in this book of 'lost' railways – opened to passengers at least three times (four times if you count those few days in 1928) it is worthy of celebration 'for that which was lost is again found'.

*Southbury station; view northwards towards Cheshunt. European steam survivor preserved in the adjacent yard of the Enfield Timber Company. (Author)*

# Angel Road to Lower Edmonton

Lower Edmonton station on the line to Enfield and Cheshunt via Southbury has a more complicated history than most. The present station is in fact the newer high-level part of the original station which came into existence in 1849 as an intermediate station on the line to Enfield from Edmonton (now Angel Road) station on the Eastern Counties Railway's main line (opened in 1840) up the Lea Valley towards Cambridge.

This line resulted from the fact that the Eastern Counties Railway, in its anxiety to find a nice level route out of London, had followed the flat valley, bypassing the old market town of Enfield a few miles to the west. The residents of Enfield and Edmonton had not been happy and petitioned the ECR for something better. Edmonton folk were not overjoyed that the station that bore the name of their village was actually some distance away on the edge of the damp and dangerous marshes at Angel Road. Enfield just wanted a station!

*The footpath leading from the Edmonton Green shopping centre towards Angel Road follows the route of the old GER line. (Author)*

159

At Enfield as at Staines (GWR) an existing house – one with some pedigree – was pressed into service. A three-storey late 17th century house which had latterly been a school attended by John Keats was taken over for the station house and offices.

Some people are never satisfied. It was not long after the line opened that complaints began about the circuitous route via Angel Road (formerly Edmonton) and Stratford that trains were obliged to take to get to Bishopsgate (at that time the London terminus before the extension to Liverpool Street was opened). A more direct route was needed but the Great Eastern Railway (successors to the Eastern Counties) had big financial problems and it was not until 1872 that the direct line via Stamford Hill and Hackney Downs was completed. Enfield was now only ten miles by rail from the City rather than nearly fifteen.

Sadly for those with an appreciation of architecture, the scheme also saw the demolition of the historic station building at Enfield with its beautiful façade and tracery work in carved brick 'unrivalled in England' according to one writer. However, the central part of this frontage was taken down carefully for preservation at the Victoria & Albert Museum.

Lower Edmonton had now become a junction with two parts to the station – the 'high-level' platforms on the new direct line via Hackney Downs and the 'low-level' station on the original line to Angel Road. This latter now became somewhat redundant although some workmen's trains starting at Lower Edmonton did go that way, as did some goods trains. A small booking office on the platform issued weekly or fortnightly blocks of the special cheap tickets – required by Act of Parliament as the cost of not requiring the railway company to rehouse the large number of poor working-class people displaced by the construction of Liverpool Street station. There was a legal requirement for a 2d return train to be run daily from Lower Edmonton to London (and on several other routes, although this was opposed in some areas where residents feared it might 'lower the tone' of the district if the working-class could afford to live there).

By 1908 there were five trains a day via Angel Road at 2d and also some faster trains on which the fare was 3d but after the First World War the number of passengers had dropped considerably and the service began to be reduced. Nearly

*GER train at Edmonton Low Level station, c1880. (Enfield Council Local History Unit)*

everyone now travelled on the newer line and in 1931 the solitary morning train via Angel Road was withdrawn. Curiously the corresponding evening train from London was not withdrawn until 8th September 1939.

After that the Lower Edmonton–Angel Road section was mainly used by goods trains. No passenger trains were to be seen unless engineering works or other problems resulted in diversions off the direct route. This particularly happened during the 1950s when other lines in the area were being electrified under the Modernisation Plan.

The low-level station at Lower Edmonton was still in place – a strange survival and not at all in keeping with the ideals of the modernisers. There was just a single track but two platforms separated by a level crossing. Approaching by train from Angel Road you first came to a platform of standard height, built in about 1900 and used for just thirty years. By 1959 this platform had no buildings and, apart from some derelict lamp-posts had no other structures on it. Access to this platform for passengers was from the level crossing.

On the other side of the level crossing, towards Enfield, was

*Lower Edmonton low-level platform, 1965. View towards Angel Road. (Enfield Council Local History Unit)*

the original platform and station building, dating from 1849. This platform was very low and had steps cut into it about halfway along to give access to a public footpath which crossed the track here. When a passenger train was alongside the platform the steps had to be covered with a board. It sounds a most Heath Robinson arrangement.

During the period when trains were diverted along the Angel Road route due to the electrification work a few station nameboards had to be hastily borrowed from the high-level platforms and attached to the lamp-posts on the low-level platform. Passengers still had to buy the tickets at the normal booking office in the high-level station but were, at least, provided with a temporary waiting room in the old station building at the lower level. However, by 1964, the electrification completed, all this was no longer needed, the old route was closed to all traffic and the tracks lifted the following year.

Trains continue to run at frequent intervals between Liverpool Street and Enfield Town through the high-level platforms at Lower Edmonton but of the original low-level station there is no

162

*Enfield Town. (Stations UK)*

trace. The route of the line lay through the site of the modern Edmonton Green shopping centre. From there a footpath still leads south-eastwards towards Angel Road and is much used by residents of the nearby flats. It occupies a broad strip of land which gives the game away that this is the course of the former railway, although there are no other clues to its short-lived existence. On the opposite side of Montagu Road large advertising hoardings block the way but the former trackbed can be seen at the end of Rays Avenue or Rays Road. Here a massive metal scrapyard dominates the scene, hardly an attractive outlook for the nearby houses. The pedestrian walking up the Conduit Lane flyover towards the entrance to Angel Road station gets a good view of the overgrown track pointing back towards Edmonton Green. The circuitous path that leads eventually to the platforms of Angel Road is built over the last few yards of the old route.

Only a short section of 'lost' line then, a curious little quirk in local railway history.

# Wood Green to Enfield

Across what is now the London Borough of Enfield the Great
Northern Railway opened a branch from Wood Green to Enfield
in 1871. Construction of the line did not go without a hitch. The
winter rains cracked a culvert carrying a stream through one of
the embankments and there was a landslip. Bad weather
hindered construction of the stations and the opening of the line
was delayed by several weeks, finally taking place on April 1st, a
date which caused some wry amusement locally. All went well
although the previous night residents in the area were terrorised
by a series of explosions along the line. This turned out to be
some of the navvies letting off fog detonators to celebrate the
completion of their contract.

Another landslip caused further problems, however, and for a
while it seems, timorous passengers were prone to ask whether it

*GNR's Enfield terminus on Windmill Hill, 1898. (Enfield Council Local
History Unit)*

would be safe to travel by train to Enfield!

The GNR station was on a road called Windmill Hill to the west of the town centre. The station house was at street level, a two-storey twin-gabled house, built across the end of the platforms, emphasising the station's status as a terminus. This was somewhat curious because the line had been envisaged as part of a Wood Green-Hertford-Stevenage loop to take pressure off the main line through Hatfield.

When, in 1898, it was decided to extend the Enfield line northwards the GNR found it had a problem. Not only was Enfield station built as a terminus, to extend north from there would require a level crossing over Windmill Hill which would be an inconvenient bottleneck.

Instead it was decided to start the new line about half a mile south of Enfield at a new station to be called Grange Park. The new tracks ran slightly to the east of the old and a new Enfield

*Enfield GNR terminus, later bypassed and replaced by Enfield Chase station. (Lens of Sutton)*

*Enfield GNR terminus. View towards London. (Lens of Sutton)*

station was built alongside the erstwhile terminus. It was at a somewhat higher level and Windmill Hill was crossed on a bridge. Beyond, the new line, opened in stages from 1909, stretched northwards into Hertfordshire, built to main line specifications – the last main line to be built in England.

But what of the old Enfield terminus? The tracks remained in place and the station became a general goods depot and supplied coal brought in by rail to houses throughout the district, which was now seeing extensive suburban development. It even had a brief and unexpected rebirth as a passenger terminus in October 1940, when an unexploded bomb blocked the through route north and the old island platform was brought back into use.

In 1962 the goods yards at the other stations in the area were closed under the Beeching rationalisation scheme and the yard at Enfield (by now Enfield Chase) became the coal depot for an even wider area, stretching from suburban Palmers Green and Winchmore Hill out into still-rural Cuffley and Bayford.

However, the demand for old-fashioned solid fuel was falling fast and in 1974 the yard closed. The tracks were taken up the following year.

There is nothing left to see of the little GNR appendix from Grange Park to Enfield's former GNR terminus. Gladbeck Way now winds where the railway used to run but of the old station there is no trace at all. The fact that Station Road, running south from Windmill Hill, does not actually reach Enfield Chase station (which is at the end of Grove Close) is perhaps the only clue to where the station once was.

# 14
# Never-Never Lines

A number of lines that are 'lost' in the sense that they never existed have already been referred to, such as the 'Northern Heights' tube extension beyond Edgware to Bushey Heath and the link between Shepperton and Chertsey (Chapter 3). There were a few others, in contrasting parts of Middlesex, that also never got off the drawing board.

Among the more ambitious was a line between Uxbridge and Rickmansworth via Harefield, traversing a remote region of Middlesex that remains stubbornly rural to this day.

In 1922, long after the railway map of Britain was substantially complete, the Local Development & Light Railway Company Ltd proposed that this link should be built. It promised to open up an attractive area ripe for high-class suburban development in the Metroland tradition and there was also a potential of lucrative freight traffic from the Bell United Asbestos Company's works at Harefield.

However, although construction of the line was authorised by the Ministry of Transport in February 1923 after a Public Enquiry, nothing happened. Neither the Great Western or the Great Central, to whose joint line the new route would have been connected near Denham, nor even the Metropolitan Railway itself, was prepared to make any investment in such a scheme. In November 1924 the board of the Metropolitan declined to buy land required for the scheme and the chance was lost.

The Metropolitan then carried out surveys for a possible Colne Valley route, linking Eastcote with Harefield and Chalfont St Giles, but the expensive bridges needed to cross the river and the Grand Union Canal seemed to be sufficient to deter even the most optimistic promoters.

In the end all that materialised was a short-lived halt, named

South Harefield, between Ruislip and Denham on the GWR and GCR Joint Line (now the Chiltern Line). It was opened in September 1928 with hopes of picking up passengers from the new developments spreading northwards along the Swakeleys Road from Uxbridge. These hopes proved so groundless that the halt closed again at the end of September 1931 although the goods yard remained open until 1952.

When it was proposed, just before the Second World War, to extend the Central Line service from West Ruislip (known as Ruislip & Ickenham up to 1947) to Denham, there were plans for a new station (named Harefield Road) on the same site (at the Harvil Road bridge). After the war, though, the area became protected from further ribbon development so the 'red electric trains' so loved by John Betjeman never rattled along between the fields and woods of the Middlesex–Buckinghamshire border.

An older scheme in a much more urban part of Middlesex also shared the same fate. This was the Latimer Road & Acton Railway, promoted in 1881, to improve rail links to the rapidly developing district between North Kensington and Hammersmith. It would have been a branch off the Hammersmith & City branch of the Metropolitan Railway, running a little distance south of the route of the modern A40(M) motorway, and would have run for a little over two miles to link with the Great Western main line east of Acton station.

The proposed railway's neighbours were not all that keen on helping an upstart competitor that might siphon off some of their revenues. The Hammersmith & City would only agree to an interchange platform (rather than a junction) where the two lines met at Wood Lane and the GWR insisted that the Latimer Road & Acton company build its own station at Acton instead of having access to the Great Western one.

In the end all that happened was the demolition of a house on the site of the LR&A station at Friar's Place Green, Acton and the construction of a bridge over what is now the West London Extension line near the present motorway bridge. Various proposals and modifications to the scheme continued to be put forward, including several attempts at a route between Ealing and Shepherd's Bush, but all they did was keep the surveyors and lawyers profitably employed.

169

It was not until 1912 that the line between Ealing and Shepherd's Bush was begun by the Great Western. This was not used by any regular passenger service until 1920 when it became part of the Central Line tube service. Extra stations at West Acton and North Acton were opened in 1923.

In the end this part of Middlesex did get a frequent and reliable train service but the final scheme was rather different – its route running somewhat further north than the original Latimer Road & Acton proposals.

Another proposal that did not see the light of day – for much of its route it was never intended to – came from the Central London tube railway. In the years before the Great War they were looking for possible extensions into the western suburbs from where extra passengers and revenue could be attracted. This would help the finances of the expensively-constructed section through the West End and the City. In 1912 they put forward a plan for an underground extension west from Shepherd's Bush via Goldhawk Road, Stamford Brook and Chiswick to Gunnersbury with trains running through to Richmond and perhaps beyond to Twickenham, Staines or Shepperton on existing surface tracks owned by the London & South Western Railway. Direct tube links to these areas might have accelerated their incorporation into the metropolis!

But it was not to be. The Parliamentary Act authorising the work received the Royal Assent in August 1913 but the war intervened and the plans were abandoned. Something similar was considered again in 1920, this time linking Shepherd's Bush and Richmond via Hammersmith to compensate for the withdrawal of the LSWR's Kensington (Addison Road now Olympia) to Richmond service via Shepherd's Bush. But the extension westward of District and Piccadilly Line services along the LSWR route via Stamford Brook was the cheaper option which won the day.

A station that never existed is North End between Hampstead and Golders Green on the Northern Line. This section of the line was opened in 1907 and the original plans included an underground station on Hampstead Way, near to the famous old Bull & Bush pub of Music Hall fame. Work on the station was begun and it would have had a street level building on the north side of the road, opposite Wyldes Farmhouse.

It was soon realised by the Directors of the line that the station had little prospect of stimulating lucrative residential development nearby as it was surrounded by the protected open space of Hampstead Heath. Perhaps someone had hopes of picking up the trippers' trade on high days and holidays or perhaps no one had studied the map closely enough.

In any event the proposed North End station was cancelled, despite the fact that some work had been done. The alert passenger on the Northern Line today may glimpse what appears to be the remains of a disused station but it is just North End – the station that never was!

All that has happened since is that a floodgate control room was put in at North End in the 1950s. At that time access from the street was provided for the first time although the site originally intended for the station entrance from Hampstead Way was sold for housing in 1927.

Not far away, on the other branch of the Northern Line, is a station that did exist once, but is now closed, South Kentish Town (opened 1907, closed 1924), noteworthy for being the scene of a chilling little story by John Betjeman about an absent-minded passenger who got out at the closed station and got trapped in an underground lift-shaft. This is based on an incident that actually happened soon after closure, reported in the staff magazine in the form of a poem, which Betjeman later used as the starting point for his creepy tale.

# 15

# Requiem For Broad Street

## The NLR line via Dalston Junction –
## the 'Happy Afterthought'

*The abandoned trackbed between Dalston Junction and Broad Street. View looking south from Richmond Road. (Author)*

Sir John Betjeman, who knew more about London's lost lines than anyone, wrote of Broad Street that it was the terminus which 'hardly anyone uses at all ... given over to the frock-coated citizens who once crowded the old North London trains from the steam suburbs of Highbury, Canonbury and Camden Town'.

Yet it was not always so. Around 1900 there were more trains arriving at Broad Street than at Euston and Paddington put together. Trains came in from Wolverhampton and Birmingham

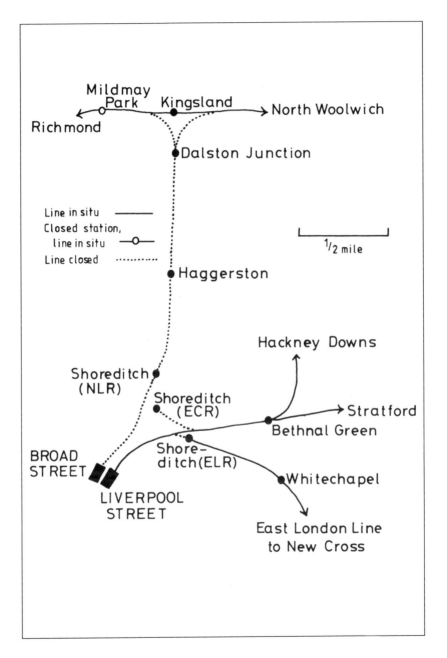

– a celebrated 'City to City' service which boasted an army of lady typists on board, ready to do letters for a small fee. There were seven platforms and each day nearly 800 arrivals brought 85,000 passengers into the station, in the shadow of its more famous neighbour, Liverpool Street. Many of the lost railway services of Middlesex terminated at Broad Street: North London Railway trains ran to destinations as diverse as Alexandra Palace, Edgware via Finchley Church End (later Finchley Central), Poplar, Blackwall, Kingston via Hampstead Road and Twickenham, Hammersmith & Chiswick via Acton, Stratford, Enfield, Palmers Green and Kew Bridge among others.

The North London Railway, whose terminus it was, was part of an ambitious scheme to link the Thames to north London and Birmingham. The first section to open, in September 1850, ran from Bow Junction to Islington and the route was extended to Hampstead Road (subsequently known as Primrose Hill station and now closed). In 1852 the line from Poplar to Bow was opened and freight services ran to and from the West India Docks. Coal was brought in by sea and delivered by rail throughout suburban north London.

Traffic grew and it was decided to run directly into the City from Dalston. It was an expensive two miles to construct as it was largely on an impressive viaduct but the new link was so successful that it became known as the 'Happy Afterthought'.

Broad Street station was opened with great ceremony in 1865. It was a grandly-decorated brick, granite and terracotta edifice whose inauguration was attended by the Lord Mayor and Sheriffs of the City of London. The North London Railway Company had great pretensions but also a quirky resistance to changing fashions. Betjeman once recalled that 'the North London was the last line to use wooden-seated third-class carriages, as it did on its Poplar branch; the last line in London to run no trains during church time on a Sunday morning and within living memory the General Manager of the line refused to allow Smith's bookstall at Broad Street to sell any vulgar-looking papers.'

The company established a locomotive works at Bow in 1863 which in its heyday covered over thirty acres. There is nothing left to see now. The area was heavily bombed during the Second

World War and, although the repair of wagons continued at Bow until the mid 1960s, the site has been totally redeveloped. One surviving relic, though, is NLR tank engine no 116 which is preserved on the Bluebell Railway in Sussex.

Sir John's affectionate account of the idiosyncrasies of the North London was written before nationalisation of the railways in 1947 but even then the great days of Broad Street were long gone. The intermediate stations, Shoreditch and Haggerston, were damaged in the Blitz and closed to passengers in 1940. The passenger service from Dalston to Poplar was ended in May 1944. All that remained of the once-proud NLR were 'those sumptuous LMS electric trains that swing across the North London suburbs on that smooth, useless, beautiful journey to Richmond' and a suburban service to Watford.

By the early 1980s the Richmond service was all that was left. The station catered for a mere 4,000 passengers a day and was in bad condition. The decision was taken to close Broad Street station and to redirect the Richmond service to North Woolwich, along former North London tracks, providing new or reopened stations at Dalston Kingsland, Hackney Central, Homerton and Hackney Wick and improving transport links into the Docklands area whose regeneration was just beginning.

Not long before the closure of the 'Happy Afterthought', the writer Alexander Frater visited the decaying terminus for his series 'Stopping Train Britain' which appeared in the *Observer* magazine. It was a poignant experience: '...at the foot of the grand central staircase – now soiled and unswept – there was a small porno shop.' (What would the late lamented General Manager recalled by Betjeman have made of that?) 'Upstairs on the main concourse, by contrast, stood a memorial to the North London men who fell in the Great War.'

He goes on to describe travelling out of Broad Street on the Richmond service, all that was left of the North London Railway's legacy: 'We ran along a tall embankment, the dowdy houses, shops and small factories of Bishopsgate stretching away on either side, the glittering towers of the City rising up behind like the battlements of some fabulous medieval fortress...'

His description of the rest of the journey to Richmond still cannot be bettered and this line, once threatened with becoming

175

'lost', is now a vital part of the London railway network and is shown on the London Underground maps. On some stretches and at some of its less-frequented stations it retains to this day just a hint of the atmosphere of the lost suburban railways of Middlesex.

Although most of the North London route remains open, the four-track section from Dalston Junction to Broad Street did succumb. However, its elevated route, mostly carried on the low arches of the Kingsland viaduct, cutting a swathe through the densely built-up districts of Dalston and Haggerston, does not need great detective skills to retrace because its structures remain virtually intact.

Exploration of the line is most easily accomplished on foot from the North London line. From an eastbound train the remains of the platform of the long-closed Mildmay Park station can be seen on the south side of the line just after leaving Canonbury. Soon afterwards, also on the south side of the line, the wide trackbed curves away in the direction of Dalston Junction and the terminus. It looks eminently walkable but the land remains railway property and the entrances to the short tunnels are securely fenced off.

Get off the train at Dalston Kingsland and, on leaving the station, turn right into Kingsland High Street. On the Saturday morning that I was there a bustling cosmopolitan street market was in full swing.

After the Balls Pond Road crossroads, continue heading south towards the futuristic financial towers of the City of London, only a mile or so distant but socially another world. The arches of the Kingsland viaduct can be glimpsed down the side streets and the trackbed can be easily seen from Forest Road or Richmond Road. Ornate and well-maintained original bridges span Middleton Road and Haggerston Road near the resoundingly-titled London Dog Centre (actually a modest little pet shop). In the angle between these roads, up against the Middleton Road bridge, is a small brick building which looks as if it might be the entrance to the former Haggerston station. A short detour along Haggerston Road brings you to a delightfully quiet little oasis, almost a village green, quite a surprise in this bustling district.

Shortly afterwards both the Kingsland Road and the railway's route cross the Regent's Canal. Most of the decking of the railway bridge was removed after closure to forestall foolhardy trespassers. However, the side of the bridge facing the road bears the neatly-stencilled, if somewhat baffling legend, 'Please Drive By Carefully In Our Village'. Not far beyond the slim and elegant minaret of a newly-built mosque adds an oriental aspect to the area. Just down the road, Christ's Apostolic Church boldly proclaims the need for 'Prayer and Salvation'.

A little beyond the attractive low buildings of the Geffrye Museum on the left, the Kingsland Road is crossed at an angle by the massive girder bridge that carried the railway. This domineering structure has remained intact since the line's closure in 1986.

Shoreditch (North London Railway) station was away to the right at the Old Street junction. Confusingly there were three stations that bore the name Shoreditch, all in different locations and built by different companies: the original terminus of the

*Viaduct taking the line to Broad Street over the Regent's Canal. The decking of the bridge has been removed to deter intrepid trespassers. View looking west. (Author)*

*Curious stencilled message on the bridge crossing the Regent's Canal. View looking east. Dalston is to the left; Broad Street is to the right. (Author)*

Eastern Counties Railway (later the Great Eastern) which was superseded by Liverpool Street, the North London station and the terminus of the East London Line from New Cross.

Incidentally, it is worth diverting to the left down Bethnal Green Road to Brick Lane to find the primitive-looking East London Railway Shoreditch terminus, served by trains from New Cross and Whitechapel at peak hours only and, rather bafflingly, on Sunday mornings. The sparsely-used track hides from view in a brick-lined cutting. Pedley Street and Weaver Street run alongside, in places still cobbled. The presence of a small urban farm, with Shetland ponies within half a mile of the financial heart of the City, is somewhat strange and the forlorn little station looks to be in its last days.

Back on Shoreditch High Street (the continuation of Kingsland Road), the old Great Eastern Bishopsgate Goods Depot (briefly the passenger terminus of the Eastern Counties Railway) is on the left and the occasional brick arch or bridge over side roads can still be glimpsed off to the right but the route of the North

*Massive girder bridge still in situ over Kingsland Road. View looking south towards the City. (Author)*

London Railway now becomes more difficult to follow and eventually disappears at the modern Broadgate development. This was built on the site of Broad Street station, a prime commercial site on the northern edge of the Square Mile. It seems in all senses to be the End of the Line.

But with a new century came plans for revival. Work began in late 2001 on a northern extension to the Metropolitan's East London Line, for long a tiny appendix to the Underground map. The new line diverges from the existing ELR north of White-chapel and will make use of the old North London track back to Dalston Junction. The former ELR Shoreditch station off Brick Lane will be closed and replaced by a new station at Bishopsgate.

It was planned that the new line would follow the course of the viaduct which once served the original Eastern Counties Railway terminus at Shoreditch, later Bishopsgate Goods Depot. This would be demolished and part of its site given over to new office development. In early 2002, however, conservationists,

179

*Exterior of the old Bishopsgate goods depot (former ECR terminus). View from Shoreditch High Street. (Author)*

*The unprepossessing exterior of Shoreditch station – northern terminus of the LT East London line. This station is only open for limited periods during the day. It will be bypassed and closed when the new extension is completed. (Author)*

including HRH Prince Charles, English Heritage and the London Railway Heritage Society, raised objections and the older part of the viaduct, the original ECR section, was granted Grade II listing by the Culture Secretary, Tessa Jowell. The objectors continued to campaign for the whole of the structure to be protected. Then, in July 2003, the Court of Appeal rejected a challenge to the proposal and the plans were put back on track. The Grade II Braithwaites Viaduct is, of course, safe.

But whatever the outcome, Betjeman's beloved Broad Street is gone for ever!

# Conclusion

The railways of Middlesex have fared better than those of most counties. The suburban nature of the area and the congested state of its roads meant that there was always a high demand for rail transport even if the disgruntled commuters were not always impressed with the service that they received. The map of rail routes in 2003 looks very similar to that of 1903. Indeed there have been some additions, notably the Heathrow Express link from Paddington.

The lines that have been lost were those that duplicated others, often constructed in the days of wasteful inter-company rivalry: two of the three lines to Uxbridge, two of the three to Alexandra Palace, one of the two to Stanmore.

Incorporation into the London Underground network, with its frequent trains, usually ensured survival. The little loop of the District Line between South Acton and Acton Town is an exception but this was always a curiosity, the result of an historical accident, and in any case both stations remain open and see frequent trains on a variety of routes. If the Highgate to Alexandra Palace and Mill Hill East to Edgware sections had been electrified and incorporated into the tube system as planned they would probably still be open today.

There have been some closures of tube stations. The intrepid could search for traces of stations such as British Museum (Central Line), Mark Lane (District/Circle) or St Mary's, White-chapel Road (District/Metropolitan). Of some, the only evidence is the changed note of the train's rumble as it enters the wider section of tunnel where the remains of the platform lie deserted and inaccessible in the darkness. Sometimes the original surface buildings survive, converted for other uses but still recognisable. J. E. Connor's book, *Abandoned Stations on London's Underground*, is an indispensable guide to these ghostly locations.

Then there are the closed stations on surface lines that remain open to traffic. One such was Uxbridge Road on the West

London Railway, north of Kensington (Addison Road – now Olympia). In its heyday it was served by West London Railway trains between Clapham Junction and Willesden Junction and also by Metropolitan Railway services that reached it via a connecting spur off the Hammersmith & City route near Latimer Road, calling also at Addison Road and Earl's Court. This was the so-called Middle Circle route which survived until 1940. Indeed it was, rather confusingly, still shown on the London Transport pocket map as late as 1947. The station's buildings at Uxbridge Road were demolished in the early 1960s.

The West London Line's history is more complex than most. For years most passengers knew it solely (if at all) for the District Line's Exhibitions Only service from Earl's Court to Olympia or British Railway's short-lived Motor Rail service. In recent years though the Clapham Junction to Willesden Junction service has been revived by Silverlink Trains and operates every twenty minutes for much of the day.

New services using existing routes – and even new lines – offer the prospect of a rail revival, although there have been too many false dawns for there to be total optimism. The East London Extension will shortly bring trains back to that broad swathe of viaduct through Kingsland and Haggerston. Extensions to the Docklands Light Railway continue. Building of the new link to Lewisham resulted in the original section of the DLR through Mudchute and Island Gardens (opened in August 1987) being abandoned in January 1999. This section is on a low viaduct, built originally for the Millwall Extension Railway in 1871 and first closed in 1926. Now disused for the second time, the viaduct is a listed structure and has to be preserved. DLR trains to Lewisham use a new alignment nearby and there are replacement stations named Mudchute and Island Gardens.

There are new possibilities west of London too. Access is notoriously bad to Heathrow Airport from the south and the future may yet see new railways from Feltham and/or Staines. In June 2003 I took part in a demonstration in Harmondsworth protesting about plans for a third runway at Heathrow which would obliterate much of the village, along with Sipson and Harlington. Should such a disaster happen (heaven forbid!) would the new terminal need extra rail links?

183

Another controversial project is the so-called Central Railway scheme. Privately-promoted, it envisages a route for freight from the North and the Midlands bypassing London by running parallel with the M25. Part of the environmentally-sensitive area of Staines Moor would have to be taken and homes demolished elsewhere on the proposed route. Householders in the affected areas are already complaining vociferously about the effects of 'planning blight'.

Doubtless some of Middlesex's lost lines that have mouldered into disuse and obscurity were also opposed by local residents out to thwart the high hopes of the lines' promoters. The term 'nimbyism' had not been dreamt of then, nor 'concern for the environment'. These railways, even those that have been totally obliterated, changed the face of their districts for ever – for better or worse!

184

# Opening and Final Closure Dates of Lines to Regular Passenger Traffic

Dates refer to regular timetabled passenger services. Some of these lines were used for goods traffic, excursions and the occasional engineering diversions for several years more. Full details in the individual chapters.

| Line | Opened | Final Closure |
| --- | --- | --- |
| Angel Road–Lower Edmonton | 1849 | 1939 |
| West Drayton–Uxbridge (Vine Street) | 1856 | 1962 |
| South Acton–Hammersmith & Chiswick | 1858 | 1916 |
| Southall–Brentford | 1860 | 1942 |
| Dalston–Broad Street | 1865 | 1986 |
| Finsbury Park–Highgate | 1867 | 1954 |
| Mill Hill East–Edgware | 1867 | 1941 |
| Kensington (Addison Rd)–Hammersmith Grove | 1869 | 1916 |
| Enfield GNR spur | 1871 | 1910 |
| Highgate–Alexandra Palace | 1873 | 1954 |
| Seven Sisters–Palace Gates | 1878 | 1963 |
| Hounslow Town spur | 1883 | 1909 |
| West Drayton–Staines West | 1884 | 1965 |
| Harrow & Wealdstone–Stanmore | 1890 | 1964* |
| Lower Edmonton–Cheshunt | 1891 | 1909** |
| South Acton–Acton Town | 1899 | 1959 |

| | | |
|---|---|---|
| MWB Railway, Kempton Park | | |
| (approx dates) | 1915 | 1940*** |
| Denham–Uxbridge (High Street) | 1907 | 1939 |
| Wembley Exhibition Loop | 1924 | 1969 |

* Belmont–Stanmore closed 1952
** Reopened 1960
***This line did not carry passengers

# Bibliography

Baker, I. & Connor, J.E. *The Stanmore Village Branch* (Connor & Butler)

Barker, J.L. & D.M. *Snapshots of Staines* (Borough Books)

Connor, J.E. *Abandoned Stations on London's Underground* (Connor & Butler)

Connor, J.E. *Finsbury Park to Alexandra Palace* (Middleton Press)

Connor, J.E. *The Tottenham Joint Lines* (Connor & Butler)

Connor, Piers *Going Green – The District Line* (Capital Transport)

Conolly, W. Philip *British Railways Pre-Grouping Atlas and Gazetteer* (Ian Allan)

Croome, Desmond F. *The Piccadilly Line* (Capital Transport)

Davis, Reg *Rails to the People's Palace* (Hornsey Historical Society)

Dix, B.K. *Staines Past and Present* (Ad Pontes Books)

Edwards, Dennis & Pigram, Ron *The Golden Years of the Metropolitan Railway and the Metroland Dream* (Bloomsbury Books)

Frater, Alex *Stopping Train Britain* (Hodder & Stoughton)

Harper Collins (pub) *London: The Photographic Atlas*

Heselton, Kenneth Y. *The Metropolitan Water Board Railway in Sunbury – Echoes From The Past*, Volume One (Sunbury & Shepperton Local History Society)

Hodge, Peter *The Hertford Loop* (Southgate Civic Trust)

Horne, Mike & Bayman, Bob *The Northern Line* (Capital Transport)

Jackson, Alan A. *London's Local Railways* (David & Charles; revised edition – Capital Transport)

Klapper, Charles *London's Lost Railways* (Routledge & Kegan Paul)

Lake, G.H. *The Railways of Tottenham* (Greenlake Publications)

Leigh, Chris *The Western Before Beeching* (Ian Allan)

Marshall Cavendish (pub) *Railway Walks*

Mitchell, Vic & Smith, Keith *The Kingston and Hounslow Loops* (Middleton Press)

Mitchell, Vic & Smith, Keith *Branch Lines of East London* (Middleton Press)

Mitchell, Vic & Smith, Keith *Branch Lines of West London* (Middleton Press)

Robbins, R. Michael *The North London Railway* (Oakwood Press)

Rolt, L.T.C. *Red for Danger* (Pan Books)

Smithers, M. *Staines – An Illustrated Record* (Ian Allan)

Welbourn, Nigel *Lost Lines – London* (Ian Allan)

Also numerous articles in *Great Western Railway Journal, Great Western Railway Magazine, Journal of Transport History, The London Railway Record, Railway Magazine, Railway World, Trains Illustrated* and other railway enthusiasts' publications.

Two websites were particularly valuable sources of information and pictures:
www.freespace.virgin.net/p.sillwood/Transport
www.magma.ca/~dewi/tranins/stanmore/stanmore.html

# INDEX

189